From the Garden

From the Garden

HATTIE KLOTZ

PHOTOGRAPHY BY LEIGH CLAPP

NEW HOLLAND

CONTENTS

INTRODUCTION

Food comes first. It's the first thing I think of when I roll out of bed in the morning. It was the first question my father asked my mother at breakfast when I was a child: 'What's for dinner tonight?' Her answer guided his choice of wine, pulled up from the cellar below, and later in the day, the vegetables he would bring in from the garden. Piles of earthy new potatoes, prickly courgettes, crunchy beans, hilariously-shaped carrots, multi-coloured beetroots, peas, broad beans, cucumbers, tomatoes, parsnips, artichokes, rhubarb and more piled high in the kitchen sink. Every day, we ate at least four different vegetables harvested less than two hours before they appeared on the table.

Now, some 30 years later, dinner is still the first thing that crosses my mind as the light seeps in, too early each morning. What are we going to eat for dinner tonight? Usually I cook twice—once earlier in the evening for my three young children—and later for my husband and I and any guests. To a certain degree we all eat the same thing. The one constant is that we all eat lots of vegetables. Indeed, this apple did not fall far from the tree at Pashley Manor Gardens.

The award-winning gardens at Pashley have been open to the public for over 20 years. And while I've loved the tulip festivals, the magnificent roses and lost myself in the scent of lilies, it's the well-ordered and incredibly productive kitchen garden that brings me back time and again. During the season, the half-acre, Victorian walled garden produces enough food to feed hundreds of guests in the garden restaurant, and a cornucopia of goodness for anyone staying in the house overnight.

The garden's soft pink brick walls radiate heat in the summer months, ripening the berries, pears, figs and tomatoes that grow alongside them. They contain neat, row upon row of vegetables, and bristling heads of parsley, bushels of thyme, rosemary, chives and other herbs. Occasionally they shelter the odd rabbit that wreaks untold damage overnight, but mostly they offer protection to good, delicious things to eat.

My parents have cooked with all these good, fresh things for years. Slap a bunch of leeks on the countertop before my mother and she'll rattle off ten delicious things to make with them. Just a few hours after a recent trug of gooseberries appeared in the kitchen, she produced a gooseberry mousse, paired with a jelly made from sparkling wine in which whole fruit floated like balloons in a summer sky.

This book captures some of the best recipes prepared with produce from the gardens, served in the café and enjoyed at the family kitchen table at Pashley Manor.

CHAPTER 1

LEEKS, ONIONS, GARLIC AND SHALLOTS

Leeks are my favourite vegetable. They taste good in everything. They're mild and sweet but add an unmistakable, oniony depth to any dish they grace. They're easy to cook, clean and prepare and they don't make you cry. They're even pretty to look at and low on waste. Discard the rooty ends and the coarse, dark green bits at the other end, but keep any pieces you don't use for your recipe (as long as they're not muddy), and throw them into a stockpot with your chicken bones.

Growing tips: Despite the fiddly business of starting under cover and then planting out, leeks are easy to grow and pest-resistant. The most important thing to keep in mind is that the more of the leek that's underground, the longer the white part you'll get. In the garden at Pashley Manor, they use a tool called a dibber, to make a 15-centimetre (6-inch) deep hole for the baby leek. Trim the roots and the top, drop it into the hole and fill with water. Don't touch until you're ready to harvest. Sprintan, Musselburgh, Swiss Giant and Toledo are some varieties to try in your own garden.

ONION AND CIDER SOUP

Serves 4

INGREDIENTS
knob of butter
2 tablespoons olive oil
3 white onions, sliced
2 medium potatoes, peeled and chopped into rough chunks
2 Bramley apples (or other tart, cooking apple, if unavailable),
  peeled, cored and roughly chopped
330 ml bottle dry apple cider
750 ml/24 fl oz chicken stock
salt and pepper
handful fresh thyme, chopped

To serve
4 slices toast (sourdough)
115 g/4 oz strong cheese, grated

METHOD

❋ Melt the butter and olive oil in a large saucepan. Add the onions and potatoes. Sweat over a medium heat until soft. Add the apples and cook for a further 3 minutes, or until soft. Pour in the apple cider, allow to bubble for 30 seconds. Add the chicken stock and simmer for 15 minutes.

❋ Liquidise the soup with a stick blender or in a food processor and return to the saucepan to keep warm. Taste for salt and pepper. Meanwhile, cover the toast slices with grated cheese. Heat under the grill until the cheese has melted and browned slightly.

❋ Serve the soup decorated with chopped thyme and the toast, either on the side, or floating on the soup.

LEEKS AND SMOKED CHICKEN WITH A HERBY CRUST

Serves 4

This is comfort food at its gourmet best. It might not be the thing to serve at a dinner party, but it's perfect for kitchen supper or family dinners. Children love it, hungry men love it, cooks love it because you can get creative and throw in anything that tickles your tastebuds, really.

INGREDIENTS

1 serving white sauce (recipe in Need-to-know Basics at the back of the book)

2 medium potatoes, peeled

2 smoked chicken breasts

2 rashers of bacon or 2 slices of ham

4 leeks

175 g/6 oz green peas

110 g/4 oz dry breadcrumbs

1 large sprig rosemary, chopped

2 large sprigs thyme, chopped

METHOD

※ Preheat oven to 190°C/375°F

※ Make the white sauce and set aside in a warm place.

※ Cut the potatoes into medium dice. Add them to salted, boiling water and cook for approximately 7 minutes, until tender but firm. Drain and set aside.

※ Cut the smoked chicken breasts into pieces that are a similar size to the potato dice.

※ Meanwhile, cut the bacon into small pieces using scissors and add to a frying pan over medium heat. Remove roots and dark green ends from leeks and slice the white and pale green parts into medium rounds. Add to the bacon and allow to sauté gently for 2 minutes. Add the frozen peas and cook until any water has evaporated (about 2 minutes), then add the diced potatoes and allow them to brown slightly, moving the mixture about the pan so that it does not stick and burn. Add the smoked chicken dice and toss in the warm pan. Remove from the heat. Add the mixture to the white sauce and combine so that everything is covered. Pour into a baking dish.

※ Combine the breadcrumbs, rosemary and thyme. Spread over the chicken mixture and return to the oven until golden brown and the dish is bubbling. Serve immediately.

※ This recipe can also be prepared with hot smoked trout fillets, turkey or leftover roast chicken pieces. Make sure that your turkey or chicken pieces are fully cooked before incorporating them in this recipe.

LEEKS SAUTÉED IN SHERRY

Serves 4

These leeks are delicious served with a Sunday roast. Lamb or beef would be perfect; the slightly tangy, sweet and sticky sauce pairs nicely with these two meats.

INGREDIENTS
8 medium leeks
2 tablespoons olive oil
pinch of salt
250 ml/8 fl oz dry sherry
55 g/2 oz soft brown sugar
60 ml/2 fl oz beef, chicken stock or water

METHOD
✳ Clean your leeks, chopping off the rooty ends and the dark green part at the other end. Wash and check for mud.
✳ Choose a wide mouthed sauté pan, add the olive oil and leeks over a medium heat. Once they have browned slightly on one side, turn them over. Season with the salt. Once the second side has browned, pour the sherry over, add the sugar and allow it to bubble. Then add the stock. Cover the pan and allow it to simmer for 7–10 minutes, or until the root end is soft when poked with a metal skewer.

CARAMELISED LEEK SOUP

Serves 4

This is a soup for supper or a chilly winter's day. It's a subtle version of French onion soup, making leeks the star.

INGREDIENTS

2 tablespoons olive oil
2 large carrots, peeled and roughly chopped
2 large potatoes, peeled and roughly chopped
10 medium leeks, chopped into medium slices
1.5 litres/50 fl oz chicken or vegetable stock
dash of olive oil
knob of butter
115 g/4 oz demerara sugar
salt and freshly ground black pepper
2 tablespoons chopped chives
2 tablespoons whipping (thickened) cream

METHOD

❋ Pour the olive oil in a saucepan over medium heat. Add the carrot and potato. Sweat the vegetables and do not allow them to brown.

❋ Clean your leeks. Throw away the really green and dirty ends. Keep the middling green parts and the pure white ends. Put the white ends aside and add the pale and middling green parts to the other vegetables in the saucepan. Cover and allow to sweat, stirring occasionally, until soft and the slightest golden-brown tinge develops.

❋ Add the stock, simmer for 15 minutes and then liquidise with a stick blender or in a food processor.

❋ In a separate pan, add a dash of olive oil and a knob of butter. Then add the white part of the leeks and allow to soften. Once soft, add the sugar and a generous amount of freshly ground black pepper. Allow the leeks to reduce over a low heat until caramelised and brown.

❋ To serve, reheat the liquidised soup. Season with salt and pepper to taste. Stir the caramelised leeks through the soup, garnish with chives, add a dash of cream and serve.

LEEK AND CRAB TART

Serves 6–8

Try this sophisticated variation on a simple quiche—perfect for a summer lunch. Serve it with a vibrant green salad.

For a 23 cm/9 in tart pan crust
230 g/8 oz plain flour
1 teaspoon salt
2 medium garlic cloves, finely chopped
6 tablespoons extra virgin olive oil
1 tablespoon water

For the filling
small knob of butter
dash of olive oil
1 large or 2 medium leeks, cleaned
2 large eggs
1 egg yolk
240 ml/8 fl oz milk
pinch of salt
freshly ground black pepper small handful
  chopped parsley
250 g/8 oz crabmeat (mostly white)
small handful chopped chives

METHOD

❊ Preheat the oven to 200°C/400°F.

❊ Sift the flour and salt into a bowl. Put the garlic into a saucepan with the olive oil and place over a low heat for 4–5 minutes, until the garlic has infused the oil. Remove from the heat and stir in the water. Pour this into the flour, stirring it to form a dough. If the dough is too crumbly, add a dash more olive oil until it will just about come together in a ball.

❊ Press the dough into a 23 cm/9 in loose-bottomed flan tin. Prick with a fork and let rest in the fridge for about 30 minutes. Then bake the piecrust for 25 minutes or until crisp in the centre. Remove and set aside to cool. Don't worry too much about any cracks—once you bake it with the filling, it will hold together enough to serve.

❊ While the pastry is cooking, melt the butter and olive oil in a frying pan over medium heat. Add the leeks and cook until soft, about 5 minutes. Remove from the heat and set aside.

❊ Mix the eggs, egg yolk, milk, salt, pepper and parsley in a bowl. Add the crabmeat, chives and the cooled leeks and mix well. Pour into the crust and bake for 25 minutes or until golden brown and slightly puffed. Serve with a green salad.

LEEK, GOAT'S CHEESE AND TOMATO TART

Serves 6–8

For the crust

230 g/8 oz plain flour

1 teaspoon salt

2 large garlic cloves, finely chopped

6 tablespoons extra virgin olive oil

1 tablespoon water

For the filling

small knob of butter

dash of olive oil

1 large or 2 medium leeks, cleaned and sliced

2 large eggs

1 egg yolk

240 ml/8 fl oz milk or cream

pinch of salt

freshly ground black pepper

small handful chopped parsley

125 g/4 oz soft white goat's cheese

2 tomatoes, sliced

METHOD

❋ Preheat the oven to 200°C/400°F.

❋ Sift the flour and salt into a bowl. Put the garlic into a saucepan with the olive oil and place over a low heat for 4–5 minutes until the garlic has infused the oil. Remove from the heat and stir in the water. Pour this into the flour, stirring it to form a dough. If the dough is too crumbly add another dash of olive oil until it comes together.

❋ Press the dough into a 23 cm/9 inch loose-bottomed flan tin. Prick with a fork and let rest in the fridge for about 30 minutes. Bake the piecrust for 25 minutes or until crisp in the centre. Remove and set aside to cool. This makes a wonderful, crumbly base, but sometimes it does just fall apart! Don't worry, the filling will hold it together.

❋ While the pastry is cooking, melt the butter and olive oil in a frying pan over medium heat. Slice the leeks and cook until soft, about 5 minutes. Remove from the heat and set aside.

❋ Mix the eggs, egg yolk, milk, salt, pepper and parsley in a bowl. Add the crumbled goat's cheese, the cooled leeks and mix well. Pour into the crust and decorate the top with the sliced tomatoes. Bake for 25 minutes or until golden brown and slightly puffed. Serve with a green salad.

LEEK, SMOKED TROUT AND DILL PARCELS

Serves 4

These delicate little parcels are delicious as a dinner starter or a light lunch with salad. They're best served with a dollop of plain yoghurt and dill sauce on the side.

INGREDIENTS

3 leeks, cleaned and sliced
2 tablespoons butter
1 tablespoon plain flour
175 ml/6 fl oz milk
large handful chopped dill
1 lemon, zest and juice
3 smoked trout fillets

salt and pepper
1 packet filo pastry

To serve
200 ml/8 fl oz full fat plain yoghurt
2 tablespoons chopped dill
squeeze of lemon juice
salt

METHOD

❋ Preheat oven to 190°C/375°F.

❋ Gently sweat leeks in a pan with a knob of butter. When leeks are soft, add the flour and stir quickly. Add the milk a splash at a time—you are aiming for a thick sauce so it doesn't leak out of the parcels. Add the chopped dill and a little lemon zest and small squeeze of lemon juice (not too much or the sauce will thin). Take off the heat, flake the smoked trout (remove any rogue bones) and stir through the sauce so it's all nicely coated. Season with salt and pepper.

❋ Melt the remaining butter. Take filo out one sheet at a time (keep the rest covered with cling film as you work so it doesn't dry out). You don't want to rip the filo otherwise your parcels will leak. Cut each sheet into four squares and paint the top of one with butter and put the next sheet on top, repeating until all four are in a stack. Add a good tablespoon full of the trout mix in the middle and scrunch up the filo pastry around it to make a shape like an old-fashioned coin purse. Paint the outside of this with butter and pop onto a greased and lined baking tray and cook until golden.

❋ Meanwhile, mix together the yoghurt, dill and lemon juice in a small bowl. Season with salt (I like Herbamare).

❋ Serve the filo parcels immediately with a fresh salad, a generous spoonful of yoghurt and dill sauce and a wedge of lemon. (Make smaller parcels for starter courses if you prefer. This amount should make six larger ones—perfect to serve one parcel and a salad for lunch.)

QUICK COCK-A-LEEKIE SOUP

Serves 4

Traditionally thickened with barley or rice and thyme, my version of this soup is a thinner, altogether less robust version. However, children love it and it seems to warm right to the soul on a chilly winter's day. The secret is in a really good, flavourful stock. An added bonus is that after you've roasted a chicken, you've probably got the other ingredients in your fridge and freezer and it will take less than 30 minutes to whip up.

INGREDIENTS
2 tablespoons olive oil
knob of butter
4 leeks, cleaned and sliced
4 medium carrots, peeled and grated
1.5 litres/50 fl oz chicken stock
salt and freshly ground black pepper
230 g/8 oz cooked chicken, shredded into small pieces

METHOD
❊ Melt the oil and butter together over a medium heat. Add the sliced leeks and grated carrots and cook gently for 5–7 minutes or until soft. Add the chicken stock and bring slowly to a simmer. Simmer for 30 minutes with the lid on. Taste for seasoning and add salt and pepper then add the shredded chicken. Serve with a thick slice of crusty bread.

RED ONION MARMALADE

Serves 4

This marmalade is useful with everything! Delicious served with cold meats, cheese, quiche, pork pies, pâté and even warm steak. You can also freeze it, which makes it very convenient when you need to give a dish a little lift.

INGREDIENTS
55 g/2 oz butter
2 tablespoons olive oil
4 red onions, sliced
125 ml/4 fl oz red wine
125 ml/4 fl oz balsamic vinegar
1 tablespoon caraway seeds
1 tablespoon mixed dried herbs
115 g/4 oz demerara sugar
salt and pepper

METHOD
✳ Melt the butter and olive oil together in a large frying pan over medium-low heat. Add the onions, stirring occasionally, and pay attention that they do not stick. Continue cooking until the onions have taken on a nutty brown colour. Add the red wine and simmer it off, about 2 minutes. Add the balsamic vinegar and simmer again for a couple of minutes. Add the caraway seed, mixed herbs, sugar and salt and pepper. Cook gently until a soft, sticky consistency, about 15 minutes.

Baked red onions

Serves 4

This is such a simple, but such a good side dish. You just need to remember to put the onions in the oven well ahead of time, as they're best when roasted long and slow. I serve them with roast meat—pork, beef and lamb—but they're also good alongside duck confit.

INGREDIENTS
2 red onions, peeled
4 tablespoons olive oil
salt
4 tablespoons balsamic vinegar

METHOD
✳ Preheat the oven to 190°C/375°F.
✳ Cut the onions in half around the circumference. Place on a baking tray. Drizzle the olive oil over the cut half. Sprinkle with salt. Place in the oven for 1 hour. After an hour, drizzle with the balsamic vinegar and bake for a further hour.
✳ Serve warm, with the addition of more oil and vinegar if you like.

CHICKEN WITH 50 CLOVES OF GARLIC

Serves 4

This recipe comes from Caroline, a family friend. It puts the sweet, nutty flavour of slowly roasted garlic in the spotlight and will make you reconsider garlic as a background flavour.

INGREDIENTS
110 g/4 oz butter
1 large chicken, 900 g/2 lb or more
50 cloves of garlic, peeled
2 tablespoons chopped herbs such as rosemary, oregano, thyme, parsley
salt and freshly ground black pepper
2 tablespoons olive oil

METHOD
❋ Preheat oven to 150°C/300°F.
❋ Slice the butter finely and gently ease a couple of pieces under the skin of the chicken on each side so that it sits against the breasts. This will help to keep the meat moist. Slice 4 cloves of garlic in half and add to the chicken cavity with the herbs and some salt and pepper. Place the chicken in a roasting pan.
❋ Melt the remainder of the butter. Toss the remaining cloves of garlic in olive oil and butter and scatter around the chicken in the roasting pan. Cover with tinfoil and bake for 2 hours, or until juices run clear.
❋ Remove the chicken from the roasting pan and set aside in a warm place. Pour the garlic cloves and any pan juices into a sieve over a bowl. Rub the garlic through the sieve. This creates a thick pureed sauce to serve with the chicken. Serve with piles of fresh vegetables and roast potatoes, or a crisp green salad.

CHAPTER 2

COURGETTES, SQUASH AND CUCUMBERS

It doesn't seem to matter how few seedlings I plant, I always have too many courgettes. And squash! This year, one plant has produced twelve giant, yellow butternut squash. If only the cucumbers would do the same.

Growing tips: Courgettes are one of the early vegetables to come in from the garden; tiny, finger-sized and delicious, while squash lasts long into the autumn and through the winter. And if you've ever tasted a home-grown cucumber, you'll know that it's a totally different vegetable to those chilled ones commonly available at the supermarket. Marketmore and Burpees Bush Champion are good varieties to try for cucumbers, Tosca and Orelia for courgettes.

PAN FRIED COURGETTES WITH LEMON AND PARSLEY

Serves 4

I get easily bored with the rotation of vegetables on my plate for any given weeknight supper. Here's a simple way to make courgettes sing!

INGREDIENTS

8 small courgettes (zucchinis), preferably slightly larger than the size of your middle finger
large knob of salted butter
1 tablespoon olive oil
juice of a lemon
large handful chopped parsley

METHOD

❄ Slice the courgettes lengthwise and then across the middle. Each one should make four elongated pieces.

❄ Melt the butter in a frying pan and add the oil and as soon as it starts to sizzle, add the courgettes. Toss in the butter until they begin to brown slightly on one side.

❄ Remove the pan from the heat, squeeze in the lemon juice, stir in the chopped parsley and serve. The courgettes should remain crisp in the middle.

Courgettes stuffed with Bolognese sauce

Serves 4

This is comfort food par excellence and was a childhood staple when growing up. Now, when life means that I don't get out to my vegetable garden for a couple of days and courgettes turn from petite and green to huge marrows, I serve it to my children.

INGREDIENTS

1 tablespoon olive oil
1 large onion, chopped
2 carrots, grated
3 sticks celery, chopped
2 cloves garlic, pressed
1 tablespoon dried oregano
450 g/1 lb lean ground beef
156 ml/5.5 fl oz/1 small can tomato paste
796 ml/28 fl oz/1 large can plum tomatoes

or 450 g/1 lb fresh tomatoes from the garden, chopped
1 tablespoon ketchup
1 tablespoon balsamic vinegar
1 medium red pepper (capsicum), seeds removed and chopped
115 g/4 oz grated cheese
2 very large courgettes (zucchinis)/small marrows
salt and black pepper to taste

METHOD

✳ Preheat oven to 190°C/375°F.

✳ Heat the olive oil in a large saucepan. Add the onion and cook until soft, about 3 minutes. Then add the carrots, celery and red pepper, cook for a minute before adding the garlic and oregano. Cook for a minute or so, but do not allow the garlic to brown. Next add the ground beef and stir until most of the meat is coloured. Follow this with the tomato paste, then the canned or fresh tomatoes, cutting up the whole tomatoes with scissors as you pour them in, if using canned. Add the ketchup and balsamic vinegar. Cover and allow to simmer for 30 minutes, stirring occasionally.

✳ Meanwhile, slice the courgettes lengthwise. Scrape out the seeds from the middle using a spoon and remove enough of the centre to create a generous channel. Using a vegetable peeler, I remove a large strip from the underside of the courgette so that it is not tippy, when filled. Place on a foil-covered tray.

✳ After 30 minutes, taste the Bolognese sauce for salt and pepper then fill the cavities of the courgettes, sprinkle with grated cheese and bake for at least 40 minutes, depending on the size of your courgettes. They should be slightly soft.

✳ Serve with green salad and a chunk of crusty baguette for wiping up any sauce.

SQUASH MASH WITH NUTMEG

Serves 4

Here's a great alternative to mashed potato. An added bonus is that it's a pretty colour too. Especially good served with grilled lamb chops or pork.

INGREDIENTS

1 large butternut squash
115 g/4 oz butter
125 ml/4 fl oz crème fraîche
salt and freshly ground black pepper
nutmeg, preferably a whole nut to grate

METHOD

✳ Preheat oven to 190°C/375°F.

✳ Peel the squash, remove the seeds and chop into large dice. Put the squash pieces in a baking dish and add a small amount of water—about 2 tablespoons. Cover and bake until soft, about 30 minutes.

✳ Meanwhile, melt the butter. Remove the squash from the oven. Drain any liquid and either put it in a food processor if you like your mash consistency to be very smooth, or mash by hand if you prefer it more textured. Stir in the melted butter, crème fraîche, salt and pepper to taste. Now take a very fine grater and grate in your fresh nutmeg—the more the better!

✳ Keep warm until served.

SQUASH BAKED WITH CREAM AND PARMESAN CHEESE

Serves 4

This is a great winter, warming dish. Slightly sticky, rich and filling, it pairs really well with duck and lamb. Sophisticated enough to serve at a dinner party, as the flavour is so delicious, comforting enough to serve at a weeknight supper.

INGREDIENTS

1 large butternut squash
2 tablespoons water
175 ml/6 fl oz whipping cream
salt and freshly ground black pepper
55 g/2 oz freshly grated Parmesan cheese

METHOD

※ Preheat the oven to 190°C/375°F.
※ Peel the squash and remove seeds. Slice into large cubes. Put them in an ovenproof dish and add the water. Bake for about 30 minutes, or until tender, but not soggy. Drain any excess water. Pour in the cream, add salt and pepper and sprinkle with cheese. Return to the oven until cream begins to bubble and cheese has melted, about 10 minutes.

BUTTERNUT SQUASH SOUP WITH SAGE AND ROSEMARY

Serves 4

INGREDIENTS

1 large butternut squash

salt

2 tablespoons hemp or pumpkin oil

1 white onion, diced

1 garlic clove, minced

4–5 sage leaves, chopped

big sprig of rosemary, woody stem removed and chopped

1.5 litres/50 fl oz vegetable or chicken stock

115 g/4 oz pumpkin seeds

salt and pepper

pinch of freshly grated nutmeg

METHOD

❊ Preheat oven to 190°C/375°F.

❊ Peel and remove the seeds from the squash. Cut into large dice. Put in an ovenproof dish, add a couple of tablespoons of water, sprinkle with salt and bake for 40 minutes, or until soft.

❊ Heat the oil in a saucepan over medium-high heat and cook the onion for 4–5 minutes, or until softened (add the minced garlic about halfway through). Add the sage and rosemary and let cook for another 1–2 minutes.

❊ Add the squash, followed by the stock. Bring to a boil then reduce the heat to low and simmer for 15–20 minutes. Meanwhile, toast the pumpkin seeds under a grill or in a dry frying pan—watch they don't burn and leave to one side ready for serving.

❊ Blend the simmered soup until smooth. Season to taste with salt and pepper, and add a pinch of freshly grated nutmeg.

❊ Serve with a drizzle of oil, and garnish with toasted pumpkin seeds. You can also add a few fresh sage leaves, fried in butter.

SPICY SQUASH SOUFFLÉS

Serves 6

These individual soufflés are very easy to make and perfect for a light lunch or Sunday evening supper. Fluffy, fun and a vibrant yellow colour thanks to the squash and turmeric, they're best eaten as soon as they come out of the oven.

INGREDIENTS

extra butter for greasing the ramekins
½ a medium-large butternut squash
1 heaped tablespoon soft brown sugar
125 ml/4 fl oz milk
55 g/2 oz butter
½ teaspoon ground cumin
½ teaspoon ground turmeric

1 tablespoon self-raising flour
½ teaspoon curry powder
30 g/1 oz Parmesan cheese, freshly grated,
  plus a little bit more
1 large egg, separated
salt and pepper
1 egg white

METHOD

❊ Preheat the oven to 200°C/400°F.

❊ Rub a generous amount of butter around the inside of six 125 ml/4 fl oz ramekins.

❊ Cut the squash in half down its length, remove the seeds and fill one half with the brown sugar and about half the butter. Keep the other half of the squash for making soup or baking with cream and Parmesan cheese (see previous recipes). Place on a baking tray, cover with foil, and cook in the oven for about 45 minutes, or until soft. Allow to cool a little then scrape the flesh out of the squash and, using a stick blender or food processor, pulse until smooth. Set aside.

❊ Slowly bring the milk to a boil in a small saucepan, stir in the cumin and turmeric and set aside. Melt the remaining half of the butter and stir in the flour and curry powder. Cook over a low heat for 2 minutes, then slowly pour in the hot milk, stirring all the time. Once combined and smooth, allow this mixture to bubble very gently for 2 minutes.

❊ Stir in the squash puree and Parmesan. Next add the egg yolks, salt and pepper. Mix well.

❊ Beat the egg whites to stiff peaks and then fold them carefully into the squash mixture. As with any soufflé, you are trying to retain as much air as possible in the mixture. Divide the mixture between the ramekins, put them into a baking pan and sprinkle with grated Parmesan cheese. Half fill the baking pan with boiling water and cook in the oven for 15 minutes, or until golden and puffy.

Cooked cucumbers
with dill and crispy pan-fried trout fillet

Serves 4

The first time I tasted these cooked cucumbers, I had no idea what I was eating. Somehow, cooking this quintessential summer vegetable had never occurred to me. But it brings a whole new experience to cucumber, changing it into a rich, flavourful vegetable, rather than a summer lightweight.

INGREDIENTS

1 large cucumber

4 tablespoons olive oil

2 tablespoons butter

1 tablespoon white sugar

juice of ½ a lemon

2 tablespoons chopped dill

4 rainbow trout fillets, skin attached

salt

250 ml/8 fl oz full fat plain yoghurt

2 tablespoons chopped chives

METHOD

✳ With a peeler, remove several strips of peel from the cucumber so that you are left with a striped one. You want to have some skin for colour and texture, but too much can be tough. Slice the cucumber lengthwise from end to end. Remove the seeds. Slice each half in half lengthwise again, then cut the cucumber into short finger lengths.

✳ Put 2 tablespoons of olive oil in a frying pan, along with half the butter. Add the cucumber pieces and fry over medium heat for about 5–7 minutes. Add the sugar, stir for 30 seconds, then squeeze over the lemon juice and add the dill. Toss and set aside somewhere warm until ready to serve.

✳ In a non-stick frying pan melt the remaining butter and olive oil. Pat your fish fillets dry and sprinkle salt over the skin side. Once the oil is hot, put the fillets skin side up in the pan. Cook over medium high heat for about 2 minutes, until slightly browned. Flip and fry for a further 3 minutes, turning up the heat at the end to crisp up the skin.

✳ Mix together the yoghurt, chives and a little salt.

✳ Pile the cooked cucumber pieces in the middle of a plate. Artfully balance the trout fillet on top, add a dollop of the yoghurt and serve with boiled new potatoes.

CUCUMBER MOUSSE
WITH PRAWNS AND CHOPPED CUCUMBER

Serves 6

Creamy, rich and zinging with summer flavours, this is a perfect lunch dish or dinner-party starter when you have a glut of cucumbers. You can either make it in a large ring, or individual cocottes with the shrimp and cucumber salad alongside. Plenty of fresh bread or crispy toast is the perfect accompaniment.

INGREDIENTS
1 large ring mould of approximately 1.1 litres/38 fl oz or six ramekins

½ a large cucumber

230 g/8 oz plain cream cheese

150 ml/5 fl oz mayonnaise

½ teaspoon salt

1 teaspoon caster sugar

1 teaspoon Worcestershire sauce

2 teaspoons lemon juice

115g/4 oz cocktail prawns

2 tablespoons water

2 teaspoons gelatine

150 ml/5 fl oz thick cream

small bunch mint, chopped

small bunch dill, chopped

To serve

120 ml/4 fl oz plain yoghurt

120 ml/4 fl oz mayonnaise

1 tablespoon chopped dill

generous squeeze of lemon juice

salt to taste

½ cucumber, chopped

170 g/6 oz small, cooked fresh water prawns

bunch of watercress or samphire

METHOD
※ Oil the ring mould or your ramekins.

※ Peel the cucumber, cut in half lengthways and remove the seeds. Grate it into a sieve over a bowl and keep the juice. Mix the cream cheese, mayonnaise, salt, sugar, Worcestershire sauce, lemon juice, prawns and grated cucumber together, using a whisk. I like to add cocktail prawns to the mousse directly, so that they are hidden like tiny prizes inside.

※ Add the water to the cucumber juice and dissolve the gelatine in this liquid in a small saucepan. Heat gently so that it all melts. Add the dissolved gelatine to the other ingredients, mix.

※ Whip the cream to soft peaks. Add to the other ingredients, mix gently and pour the mixture into your moulds. Chill for at least 3 hours in the refrigerator.

※ Mix the yoghurt, mayonnaise, chopped dill, lemon juice, salt and taste. Then add the chopped cucumber and prawns. Turn out the mousse and serve with the prawn and cucumber salad and watercress or samphire.

CUCUMBER SALAD WITH RAISINS AND MINTED YOGHURT

Serves 4

This is a simple summer salad with a little twist. The raisins give a slightly unusual texture, which is great contrasted with the crisp bite of cucumber.

INGREDIENTS
1 large cucumber
125 ml/4 fl oz plain full fat yoghurt
½ tablespoon white wine vinegar
1 tablespoon white sugar
2 tablespoons chopped mint
170 g/6 oz raisins or sultanas
salt and pepper

METHOD
※ Dice the cucumber. Mix the yoghurt, white wine vinegar, sugar and mint. Stir in the cucumber and raisins. Add salt and pepper to taste.

CHAPTER 3

TOMATOES

The very best tomato is a late summer one, plucked from the bush and eaten immediately, with no embellishment. Second best is one sliced and served with olive oil, sea salt and crusty bread. Neither of these ways to enjoy a tomato are much good in a recipe book. But there are plenty of great ways to bring out the flavour of a less-than-perfect tomato; one that's gone wrinkly, is slightly bruised or just doesn't look all that enticing. You should never throw a tomato out, as there's always something delicious you can do with it.

Growing Tips: To grow tomatoes successfully, you really need the richest soil you can provide and plenty of fertiliser during the season, so I scratch in more manure as they produce fruit. I grow my tomatoes in large terracotta pots, so they're close by when I want to pick them, and I fill the bottom of the pots with a rich mix of well-rotted manure and soil. I water deeply, but infrequently. At Pashley Manor, the varieties Apero, Alicante, Fantasio and Incas are started inside in late winter, for planting out at the start of summer. They grow in a sheltered corner, alongside an ancient brick wall, which radiates heat. Pinch outside shoots to encourage better quality fruit and feed weekly with tomato feed. You'll grow plenty of delicious tomatoes for eating and cooking.

ROASTED TOMATO AND RED PEPPER SOUP

Serves 4

It's the red peppers in this soup that give it a little lift, adding a slightly sweet edge. A great way to use a glut of tomatoes and those twisty, ugly peppers that aren't so great for roasting any other way, this soup is also a crowd pleaser. It's a truly seasonal soup, best when tomatoes and peppers are fresh off the bush, ripened and warmed by the late summer sun.

INGREDIENTS

450 g/1 lb ripe summer tomatoes
4 red peppers (capsicums)
4 tablespoons olive oil
1 large white onion, chopped
1 litre/35 fl oz chicken or vegetable stock
2 tablespoons balsamic vinegar
salt and pepper
handful fresh basil leaves
cream to serve

METHOD

※ Preheat oven to 175°C/350°F.

※ Roughly chop the tomatoes and red peppers, removing any seeds that you can. Toss in a bowl with 2 tablespoons of olive oil. Spread thinly on a baking tray and roast for 45 minutes.

※ Meanwhile, heat the remaining olive oil in a large saucepan. Gently sweat the onion over a low heat for 5 minutes. Turn off and set aside until the tomatoes and peppers are done. Add the roasted vegetables and the stock to the onion. Bring to a boil and then simmer for 30 minutes.

※ Liquidise the soup with a stick blender or in a food processor. Add the balsamic vinegar and season to taste. Serve with freshly chopped basil, a dash of cream, croutons and a slice of fresh bread.

FRESH PLUM TOMATO SAUCE
WITH BBQ CHICKEN BREASTS

Serves 4

In this recipe, the chicken breasts are really just a vehicle for eating the luscious, rich tomato sauce. You could choose lamb chops, sausages or even a thick fillet of white fish. Whatever protein you choose, this simple sauce will give any weeknight supper a little lift.

INGREDIENTS
2 tablespoons olive oil
2 medium white onions, roughly chopped
3 red peppers (capsicums), deseeded and roughly chopped
2 tablespoons dried oregano
450 g/1 lb ripe plum (Roma) tomatoes
2 large handfuls basil leaves, chopped
salt and pepper
balsamic vinegar

METHOD
❋ Heat the olive oil in a saucepan over a medium heat. Add the onion and cook until soft, but not brown. Add the peppers and oregano, cook for a couple of minutes. Roughly chop the tomatoes, trying to retain as much juice as possible. Add to the pan. Simmer for 20 minutes, then add the basil.

❋ Remove from the heat and transfer to a food processor. Add salt, pepper and balsamic vinegar to taste. I like my sauce with a reasonably chunky texture, so a couple of pulses are usually sufficient.

❋ Serve with a bbq chicken breast and hot new potatoes, or freeze for use later in the winter.

TOMATO, BASIL AND GREEN OLIVE TART WITH A CRUMBLY BLUE CHEESE CRUST

Serves 8

This recipe is perfect for a summer lunch, served with a simple green salad. It's rustic and hearty, but not heavy and is a favourite in the café at Pashley Manor Gardens. The deep tomato flavour sings when paired with the crumbly crust. Just add a good bottle of rosé and clear the decks for the afternoon.

For the crust
230 g/8 oz plain flour
1 teaspoon salt
6 tablespoons extra virgin olive oil
2 large garlic cloves, finely chopped
1 tablespoon water
55 g/2 oz blue cheese

For the filling
900 g/2 lb fresh plum (Roma) tomatoes
2 tablespoons olive oil
4 large garlic cloves, thinly sliced
2 teaspoons caster sugar
30 g/1 oz butter
salt and black pepper
large handful basil leaves, finely chopped
basil leaves and green olives to garnish

METHOD

※ Preheat the oven to 200°C/400°F.

※ To make the crust, sift the flour and salt in to a bowl. Put the olive oil and garlic in a saucepan and heat gently for about 2 minutes. Add the water. Remove from the heat and pour into the flour mixture. Sprinkle the crumbled cheese on top and stir to combine. Add a dash of extra olive oil if necessary to bring it together. Press the crust into an ungreased, loose bottom, 23 cm/9 in flan tin. Bake for about 25 minutes or until crust is no longer soft in the middle.

※ To make the filling, skin the tomatoes by making a slice in the skin down one side with a sharp knife, putting them in a bowl and covering them with boiling water. After a few minutes, carefully remove the tomatoes from the water. Put on a pair of rubber gloves and slowly slide the skins off the tomatoes. Chop each into several slices and put them in a large saucepan with the olive oil and sliced garlic over a medium heat. Stir often and cook for about 20 minutes, or until you have a soft, slightly lumpy mixture. If there's lots of liquid, boil this off at the end over a higher heat. Then add the sugar and butter and stir for 2 minutes. Season with salt and pepper. Stir in the chopped basil leaves. Spread the tomato mixture into the crust base and serve garnished with remaining basil leaves and green olives.

TOMATO, ROSEMARY AND GOAT'S CHEESE RAMEKINS

Serves 4

This was one of the first dinner party dishes I learned to make, in my early twenties. I'm not sure if I'd serve it at a dinner party now—more likely for lunch with plenty of crusty bread and a green salad—but it tastes great whatever time of day you choose to eat it.

INGREDIENTS
4 ripe, medium tomatoes
4 tablespoons olive oil
4 small-to-medium cloves of garlic, finely chopped
2 large sprigs of rosemary, leaves removed and finely chopped
salt and black pepper
1 goat's cheese log with skin

METHOD
※ Dice the tomatoes. Remove any large lumps of seeds, but try to keep as much juice as possible.
※ Heat a small amount of olive oil in a small frying pan and add the garlic. Add the rosemary after a minute and cook for a couple of minutes until fragrant, but not brown.
※ Put the remaining olive oil in a bowl with the chopped tomatoes. Add the garlic and rosemary and a large pinch of salt. Divide this mixture evenly between four ramekins, leaving enough space on top for a 1 cm (0.4 in) thick slice of goat's cheese, to cover the top.
※ Put one slice of goat's cheese or two, depending on the diameter of your ramekin, on top of each and slide under the grill until golden brown and bubbling. Serve with crusty bread and a green salad.

STACKED TOMATO AND GOAT'S CHEESE SALAD WITH PARMESAN CRISPS

Serves 4

This is a tried and true combination of goat's cheese and tomatoes, but it's the presentation and differing textures that make this a stand-out salad for a special occasion lunch or dinner.

INGREDIENTS

4 large, ripe but firm tomatoes (I choose red and yellow when in season)

1 soft white goat's cheese log

4 tablespoons aged balsamic vinegar

4 tablespoons olive oil

Maldon sea salt and freshly ground black pepper

handful of chopped basil leaves

For the Parmesan crisps

1 cup grated Parmesan cheese

2 tablespoons flour

1 teaspoon paprika

METHOD

✴ Preheat the oven to 200°C/400°F.

✴ Slice your tomatoes into four slices each, discarding the top and bottom. Slice the goat's cheese log into twelve.

✴ Place a slice of tomato on the plate. Follow with a slice of goat's cheese, followed by another tomato, cheese slice and so on.

✴ For this recipe I use aged balsamic, as it is thicker, or a store-bought balsamic glaze. Drizzle the balsamic around your stack and dot the plate with olive oil, flakes of sea salt, basil and a little freshly ground black pepper.

✴ To make the Parmesan crisps, mix the dry ingredients together and spread evenly into four small piles on a non-stick baking tray. Cook in the oven until just golden and melted together. Keep a sharp eye on them as they will melt and burn quickly. Set aside to cool. Gently lift from the tray—these are very breakable—and serve propped up alongside a tomato and goat's cheese stack.

TOMATO JELLY WITH TOMATO AND PRAWN SALAD

Serves 6

In my opinion (as a child, disappointed that the jelly wasn't fruit flavoured), it's the salad served with this classic tomato jelly that makes the whole concoction come alive.

For the jelly
570 ml/20 fl oz tinned
   tomatoes
2 large strips of lemon rind
1 bay leaf
6 peppercorns
1 clove garlic, crushed but
   still whole
large pinch of salt
pinch of sugar
15 g/1 tablespoon gelatine
60 ml/2 fl oz water

freshly ground black pepper
4 medium, firm tomatoes,
   seeds removed and diced
2 tablespoons chopped
   chives

To serve
3 tablespoons olive oil
1 tablespoon tarragon white
   wine vinegar
pinch of salt
1 teaspoon sugar

1 teaspoon Dijon mustard
4 medium, firm tomatoes,
   roughly chopped
170 g/6 oz small, cooked
   fresh water prawns
2 tablespoons chopped basil
   leaves
1 bunch watercress
6 dariole moulds or 1
   medium ring mould

METHOD

※ Put the tinned tomatoes into a saucepan with the lemon rind, bay leaf, peppercorns and garlic. Add the salt and sugar and bring the mixture slowly to a boil, then reduce to a simmer for 5 minutes. Take the tomatoes off the heat and press them through a strainer into a measuring jug.

※ In a separate small bowl, combine the gelatine and water. Allow the gelatine to swell and dissolve and then add it to the tomato juice. Stir and check that there is close to 570 ml/20 fl oz of liquid. Add some freshly ground black pepper.

※ Drain any excess liquid from the chopped fresh tomatoes and mix them with the chives. Line the bottom of the ring mould or six dariole moulds with these. Pour the tomato liquid into the mould on top of the diced tomatoes and put it in the fridge to set, at least 3 hours.

※ Meanwhile, in a glass jar mix the olive oil, vinegar, salt, sugar and Dijon mustard and shake well to mix. Toss the tomatoes with the prawns, torn basil and the salad dressing mixture.

※ To serve, turn out the tomato ring by gently lowering the ring or your individual moulds into a sink of warm water—careful here, it will melt very quickly—then slide your serving plate over the top and quickly flip it over. Pile the prawn, basil and tomato salad in the centre, garnish with watercress or samphire, if you can find it.

WRINKLY ROASTED TOMATOES WITH BALSAMIC VINEGAR

This is a great way to use up any small tomatoes that have started to go wrinkly, or simply to intensify the flavour of a pretty vine. They are delicious as a light lunch or as an alfresco dinner starter in summer.

INGREDIENTS
tomatoes, one strand per person
olive oil
salt
balsamic vinegar
basil leaves
white goat's cheese

METHOD
* Preheat oven to 150°C/300°F.
* Put the tomatoes on a baking tray or glass baking dish. Drizzle with olive oil and some salt. Roast for approximately 45 minutes to one hour, until wrinkly, but not collapsed. Remove from the oven and drizzle with balsamic vinegar.
* Serve with torn fresh basil leaves, crusty bread and soft white goat's cheese.

CHAPTER 4

POTATOES

It is impossible for me to let a potato go to waste. Potatoes are the one food I'd take to a desert island—so versatile, so delicious on their own, or perfect as the supporting cast to a host of other flavours. A meal without potatoes is not complete. Here are several ideas that celebrate potatoes.

Growing tips: If you've got enough space, it's good to grow a selection of early, mid and late-season potatoes. Potatoes vary widely in texture so you'll also find it useful to plant waxy ones for salads and a more floury variety, for all-purpose uses. Try Charlotte, Lady Christl, International Kidney and Desiree varieties.

TARTIFLETTE

Serves 4

This is a traditional recipe that comes from the Haute-Savoie region of France—an area known for high mountains, excellent skiing, hearty cheese and great food. This dish, made with Reblochon, a washed-rind raw cow's milk cheese, will warm you to the soles of your feet on a cold winter night.

INGREDIENTS

900 g/2 lb potatoes
2 tablespoons olive oil
2 onions, minced
2 cloves of garlic, peeled and crushed
220 g/8 oz bacon, chopped
175 ml/6 fl oz cream
salt and pepper
1 ripe Reblochon cheese (soft when you prod it)

METHOD

❊ Preheat the oven to 200°C/400°F.

❊ Peel the potatoes, cut them into medium dice, rinse under cold water and dry them with a clean cloth.

❊ Heat the olive oil in a frying pan and cook the onions until soft. Add the garlic, toss a couple of times and then add the potatoes. Cook until golden, turning on all sides. Add the bacon bits and cook until crisp.

❊ Put the potatoes, bacon and onions in a baking dish. Pour the cream over the top. Sprinkle with salt and freshly ground black pepper.

❊ Cut the Reblochon around its girth, splitting into two flat discs. Then cut these pieces into two. Place them skin side facing up on top of the potatoes. Bake for 25 minutes or until cheese is melted and skin is beginning to crisp.

❊ Serve with a crisp green salad.

POTATO SALAD WITH MUSTARD AND GREEN ONIONS

Serves 4

INGREDIENTS
450 g/1 lb new potatoes
2 tablepoons olive oil
4 tablespoons grainy mustard
6 spring onions
handful chopped parsley
salt and freshly ground black pepper

METHOD
* Put a large pan of salted water on to boil. Add the potatoes and cook until firm, but can be pierced with a sharp knife. Do not cook until soggy.
* Drain, cut any large potatoes in half and toss in the olive oil and mustard.
* Chop the spring onions, removing the dark green ends and using the white and pale green parts. Add to the potatoes, along with the parsley. Season with salt and pepper.
* Can be served hot, warm or cold.
* For a variation on this theme, do not add mustard and replace the green onions with a large handful of chopped, fresh tarragon.

POTATOES WITH BEURRE NOIR AND SHALLOTS

Serves 4

INGREDIENTS

450 g/1 lb new potatoes

2 tablespoons olive oil

6 medium shallots, peeled and cut into quarters

125 g/4 oz salted butter

1 small wedge lemon

freshly ground black pepper

METHOD

❋ Put a large pan of salted water on to boil. Add potatoes and cook until firm, but soft enough to be pierced with a sharp knife. Do not cook until soggy.

❋ Drain, cut any large potatoes in half. Set aside.

❋ In a frying pan add the olive oil and cook the shallots until slightly browned. Add to the potatoes and toss.

❋ In a small saucepan, melt the butter and heat until it begins to turn golden brown. Pay very close attention here as it can burn easily. Remove from the heat and continue to keep the butter moving in the pan. This will be enough to turn it medium to dark brown. Add a squeeze of lemon juice and add to the potatoes. Toss well, add black pepper to taste and serve.

ROSTI POTATOES WITH CHEDDAR

Serves 4

Good rosti potatoes are hard to make. They tend to be either raw in the middle and starchy, or overly greasy and soggy. The trick is in how you handle the potatoes before you fry them.

INGREDIENTS

8 medium-sized waxy potatoes
salt and freshly ground black pepper
115 g/4 oz grated Sussex cheddar cheese (or another crumbly, aged cheddar, if unavailable)
2 tablespoons butter
2 tablespoons olive oil
2 eggs
2 tablespoons chopped chives

METHOD

❋ Bring a large pot of salted water to a boil. Add the potatoes and cook until firm, but soft enough to be pierced with a sharp knife. You do not want them to be cooked through, nor soft. Drain and put the potatoes aside to cool, preferably in the fridge, for a couple of hours.

❋ Grate the potatoes on the coarse side of a grater, skins included; they add good flavour and texture. Stir in chives, salt and freshly ground black pepper. Add the grated cheese. Mix well.

❋ Divide the mixture into four. Melt half the butter and oil in a frying pan and put two of the portions in your frying pan (if there's space) over a medium-high heat. Pat down gently with a spatula. Fry for about 4 minutes, then flip using a spatula and slide it back into the frying pan, golden side up. Cook until golden brown and crispy on both sides. Cheese should be melted and gooey in the centre.

❋ Serve with green salad leaves, a wedge of good cheddar and a couple of slices of prosciutto.

WRINKLY ROAST POTATOES

Serves 4

This is so simple, but so good. It leaves space on your cooktop for other jobs and the potatoes are flexible about heat when sharing the oven with something else. If you need the heat lower, plan for more time for the potatoes, simply turning the heat to high for 10 minutes at the end.

INGREDIENTS

450g/1 lb small potatoes

4 tablespoons olive oil

1 tablespoon dried oregano or mixed herbs

salt

2 large cloves of garlic, finely chopped

METHOD

❋ Preheat oven to 190°C/375°F.

❋ Toss the potatoes in the olive oil, herbs and a generous amount of salt. Spread in a single layer in a baking dish or on a tray. Cook for one hour (or more; if your timing is off, they're very forgiving). Add the chopped garlic halfway through and shake to turn the potatoes. Potatoes are ready when golden brown and slightly wrinkly.

POTATO AND CELERIAC DAUPHINOISE

Serves 4

The addition of celeriac here just elevates this dauphinoise from the classic recipe to something a little different, worthy of a weeknight supper party or a better glass of wine to accompany it. You can make it with cream for the decadent version, or really good chicken stock for a healthy version.

INGREDIENTS
1 medium celeriac (about 230 g/8 oz)
230 g/8 oz waxy potatoes
1 onion
2 cloves garlic
salt and freshly ground black pepper
250 ml/8 fl oz double cream
115 g/4 oz Parmesan cheese, grated

METHOD
✳ Preheat oven to 190°C/375°F.

✳ Peel both your celeriac and potatoes. Using a mandolin, finely slice the celeriac into discs. Do the same with the potatoes and onions, cutting them into rings.

✳ Start with a layer of celeriac in the bottom of an ovenproof dish. Follow this with a layer of onions, then a layer of potatoes. Crush a small amount of garlic using a press into the next layer, add a sprinkling of salt and a generous slosh of cream or chicken stock. Then repeat, until you have finished your ingredients. Make sure there's a good covering of cream on top and sprinkle with the grated cheese.

✳ Cover with tin foil and place on a tray so that you don't have to clean the oven if it bubbles over the side of the dish. Cook for 1.5–2 hours, removing the foil for the final 15 minutes to allow the cheese to turn golden brown.

✳ Delicious served with lamb, duck or steak.

CHAPTER 5

ROOTS: CELERIAC AND BEETROOT, PARSNIPS AND CARROTS

I love the onset of autumn and winter—enough with the salads! When the first frost hits, my mouth waters for celeriac and parsnips, while carrots add a hint of sweetness. That other root vegetable, the one you either love or hate—the beetroot—provides wonderful colour for summer salads and a host of health benefits.

Growing tips: Parsnips are tricky to grow successfully as they are can be hard to germinate, sown directly into the cold soil in late winter or early spring, for harvest the following autumn or winter after the first frost. But they're worth the effort for their woody sweetness throughout the winter months. However, beetroot are easy to grow, suffer from relatively few pests or diseases and offer a whole host of health benefits. You can also use their young leaves in mixed salads. Burpee's Golden, Chioggia Pink and Moneta are varieties of beets to try, while Picador is a good one to choose for parsnips.

CELERIAC REMOULADE WITH SMOKED DUCK

Serves 4

This classic French salad is so simple and a great way to introduce new flavours and textures to your diet during the winter months when green salads are simply not appealing. Crunchy and creamy all at once, it's a winner with duck or thinly sliced prosciutto. The addition of pomegranate seeds adds colour and citrus zing.

INGREDIENTS

1 large celeriac
1 lemon, juiced
90 ml/6 tablespoons mayonnaise
2 tablespoons Dijon mustard
45 ml/3 tablespoons crème fraîche
salt and pepper
2 tablespoons pomegranate seeds

METHOD

❋ Peel and grate or chop the celeriac. The pieces should be thinner than a matchstick, but they should not be floppy and fine like rice noodles or they will simply create a soggy mess. You are aiming for a salad with texture here.

❋ As soon as you've finished with the celeriac, toss in lemon juice to prevent it going brown.

❋ Combine the mayonnaise, mustard, crème fraîche and seasoning. Add the celeriac and toss. Set aside in the fridge for a minimum of 30 minutes, up to a couple of hours, for the flavours to combine.

❋ Serve with thin slices of smoked duck breast, garnish with pomegranate seeds.

CELERIAC PUREE WITH ROSEMARY LAMB CHOPS

Serves 4

It's the creamy, slightly earthy flavour of celeriac that pairs so well with red meats. This combination, with lamb, is a winner and a great alternative to mashed potatoes.

INGREDIENTS
1 large celeriac, peeled
115 g/2 oz butter
250 ml/8 fl oz crème fraîche or plain, full fat yoghurt
salt and freshly ground black pepper
nutmeg, freshly grated

METHOD
❋ Cut the celeriac into large chunks and put into a saucepan of water. Bring to the boil and cook until soft. Drain the celeriac and return them to the pan for a moment over a low heat. Shake to dry celeriac out. This will make your puree less liquid. Once some of the moisture has evaporated, move the celeriac to a food processor. Pulse a couple of times with the butter and then add the crème fraîche or full fat yoghurt. Process until smooth and creamy. Season with salt, pepper and nutmeg to taste.

PARSNIP AND CELERIAC PUREE
WITH ROAST DUCK BREAST

Serves 4

Adding parsnip to celeriac puree gives a hint of sweetness to the whole endeavour. It's one that marries well with duck breast with a salt crust.

INGREDIENTS
1 large celeriac, peeled
3 medium parsnips, peeled
175 ml/6 fl oz crème fraîche
salt and freshly ground black pepper

METHOD
※ Chop the celeriac and parsnips roughly. Place them in two separate pans of water and boil until each is tender when pierced with a knife. Drain. Combine the two vegetables and return to a pan. Shake over a low heat until some of the moisture has evaporated.

※ Put the vegetables in a food processor and pulse several times until a thick puree has formed. At this point, if you like your puree totally smooth, remove the vegetables and press them through a medium sieve to remove any fibrous bits. If you don't mind your puree slightly more textured then add the crème fraîche, pulse until smooth and season to taste.

CELERIAC, APPLE AND THYME SOUP

Serves 4

The sharp and sweet flavour of the apple pairs beautifully with the celeriac in this recipe, given a savoury lift by the hint of thyme. You can also choose a variation on this theme and substitute the apple for blue cheese, garnishing with apple instead.

INGREDIENTS

2 white onions

2 leeks, darker green parts removed

1 clove garlic

55 g/2 oz butter

2 tablespoons olive oil

salt and pepper

1 large celeriac, peeled and roughly chopped

2 carrots, peeled and roughly chopped

2 Bramley apples, peeled and chopped (or other tart, cooking apples, if unavailable)

half a head of celery, roughly chopped

1 litre/35 fl oz vegetable or chicken stock

175 ml/6 fl oz cream

1 bay leaf

sprig of thyme and 3 teaspoons of fresh thyme leaves

squeeze of lemon juice

METHOD

※ Sweat, onions, leeks and garlic in the butter and oil until soft. Season and add the celeriac, carrots, apple, celery, thyme leaves and stock. Drop in the bay leaf and sprig of thyme. Cook, at a simmer, until all the vegetables are soft.

※ Remove the sprig of thyme and the bay leaf. Pour the contents of the saucepan into a food processor (careful, hot!). Pulse until smooth. Add the cream and adjust seasoning to taste with the lemon juice, salt and pepper.

※ Serve with toasted walnut bread and a creamy blue cheese.

※ A great alternative to this is to replace the apple with Stilton cheese. Add about 175 g/6 oz after you have liquidised the celeriac and vegetables. Stir gently until melted and taste before seasoning. To serve, garnish with a few chunks of crisp, chopped apple tossed in lemon juice to prevent them from turning brown.

WHOLE ROAST CELERIAC

Serves 4

This is such a simple, delicious way to prepare this ugly vegetable. And while roasting it whole doesn't make it any more beautiful, it does enhance the nutty, earthy flavour. I encourage you to give it a try!

INGREDIENTS
1 large celeriac
olive oil
salt

METHOD
* Preheat the oven to 190°C/375°F.
* Scrub and clean the celeriac. Peel off the worst of the knobbly and woody bits where necessary. Rub the celeriac generously with olive oil and salt. Place on a baking tray and cook for at least 2 hours. Test by piercing with a skewer or a sharp knife. The celeriac is cooked when it is soft.
* Slice in quarters to serve and drizzle with olive oil. It is excellent when eaten with red meats, as an alternative to potatoes.

BEETROOT AND FRENCH BEAN SALAD

Serves 6

This recipe is all about visual appeal, offering two summer flavours that work well together and look great! You can cook beetroot in several ways, but I prefer to slow roast them if I have time, to bring out the sweetness, or to steam them, if pressed for time.

INGREDIENTS
4 medium beetroot
170 g/6 oz French beans
175 ml/6 fl oz olive oil
2 tablespoons chopped parsley
½ a lemon
sea salt and black pepper

METHOD
* Preheat the oven to 400°F/200°C.
* If you are going to roast the beets, first remove the leaves to about 2.5 cm (1 in) above the bulb. Keep them for stir-frying with garlic and olive oil. Give the beets a quick scrub under the tap to remove any mud and wrap them individually in tin foil. Put them on a baking tray. Roast for about 40 to 50 minutes, checking occasionally to see that they are not burning by opening a packet. If they are going a little too quickly, then add a dribble of water to the foil packet. Pierce with a knife to check when cooked.
* If you prefer to steam the beetroots, remove the leaves and any particularly hairy roots, scrub them and steam for approximately 30 minutes, according to the size of your vegetable.
* Once cooked, set the beets aside to cool. Once you can handle them, wearing a pair of rubber gloves, you can simply slide off the skins. Cut into large dice.
* Top and tail the beans and slice into 2.5 cm (1 in) pieces. Steam briefly for about 2 minutes, until bright green and al dente. Immediately refresh under cold running water.
* Toss the beans in half the olive oil, half the parsley, a good squeeze of lemon juice and plenty of salt and pepper. Do the same with the beetroot. Serve separately if you don't like the red of the beetroot to stain the beans or toss together and serve immediately.

BEETROOT AND GOAT'S CHEESE SALAD
WITH THYME AND PUMPKIN SEEDS

Serves 6

If you oven roast your beetroot, you can keep them in an airtight container in the fridge for several days. Then, you can throw this lovely salad together at the last minute for any surprise guests. I like to add lots of pumpkin seeds as they give such a lovely crunch to this salad.

INGREDIENTS

4 medium-large beetroot
1 tablespoon quality balsamic vinegar
3 tablespoons olive oil
½ a lemon

2 tablespoons lemon thyme, removed from
  the woody stems and chopped
175 g/6 oz pumpkin seeds
175 g/6 oz soft white goat's cheese
sea salt flakes and fresh black pepper

METHOD

※ Preheat the oven to 400°F/200°C.

※ If you are going to roast the beets, first remove the leaves to about 2.5 cm (1 in) above the bulb. Keep them for stir-frying with garlic and olive oil. Give the beets a quick scrub under the tap to remove any mud and wrap them individually in tin foil. Put them on a baking tray. Roast for about 40–50 minutes, checking occasionally to see that they are not burning by opening a packet. If they are going a little too quickly, then add a dribble of water to the foil packet. Pierce with a knife to check when cooked.

※ If you prefer to steam them, remove the leaves and any particularly hairy roots, scrub them and steam for approximately 30 minutes, according to the size of your vegetable.

※ Once they are cool enough to handle, wearing rubber gloves, slide off the skins. Cut into large dice. Toss in the balsamic vinegar, olive oil, a squeeze of lemon juice, lemon thyme, reserving a little to sprinkle across the top, and season.

※ In a dry frying pan, toast your pumpkin seeds until fragrant. Watch them carefully so that they do not burn. Set aside to cool.

※ When you are ready to eat, break the goat's cheese into chunks using a fork, scatter across the beetroot and sprinkle with the pumpkin seeds, some coarse sea salt flakes and remaining lemon thyme.

BEETROOT AND NEW POTATO SALAD
WITH GRAINY MUSTARD AND SMOKED TROUT FILLET

Serves 6

INGREDIENTS

4 medium beetroot

225 g/8 oz new potatoes

1 ½ tablespoons grainy mustard

1 ½ tablespoons runny honey

3 tablespoons olive oil

1 ½ tablespoons tarragon white wine vinegar

2 tablespoons chopped chives

salt and pepper

6 tablespoons plain, full fat yoghurt

2 teaspoons horseradish sauce

6 smoked trout fillets

METHOD

✳ Preheat the oven to 400°F/200°C.

✳ If you are going to roast the beets, first remove the leaves to about 2.5 cm (1 in) above the bulb. Keep them for stir-frying with garlic and olive oil. Give the beets a quick scrub under the tap to remove any mud and wrap them individually in tin foil. Put them on a baking tray. Roast for about 40–50 minutes, checking occasionally to see that they are not burning by opening a packet. If they are going a little too quickly, then add a dribble of water to the foil packet. Pierce with a knife to check when cooked.

✳ If you prefer to steam them, remove the leaves and any particularly hairy roots, scrub them and steam for approximately 30 minutes, according to the size of your vegetable.

✳ Once they are cool enough to handle, wearing rubber gloves, slide off the skins. Cut into large dice. Set aside.

✳ Bring a large saucepan of salted water to a boil. Add the potatoes and cook for approximately 15 minutes, or until you are able to pierce them with a sharp knife but they remain firm. Drain, set aside to cool.

✳ In a glass jar mix the grainy mustard, honey, olive oil, tarragon vinegar, most of the chives (keep some aside for sprinkling over the plate at serving) and a pinch of salt and black pepper. Shake well to emulsify.

✳ In a separate bowl mix the yoghurt and horseradish. Test for spice level—if not quite strong enough for your taste, add more horseradish.

✳ When you are ready to serve, combine the beetroot, potatoes and dressing. The beets will bleed into the potatoes, so you do not want to do this more than a few minutes before you serve it. Serve with a smoked trout fillet for each person, a dollop of horseradish yoghurt and decorate with chives.

CURRIED PARSNIP AND APPLE SOUP

Serves 6

INGREDIENTS

600 g/1 lb 3 oz parsnips, peeled and roughly chopped

4 tablespoons olive oil

55 g/2 oz butter

225 g/8 oz onions, diced

1 tablespoon mild curry paste

1 litre/35 fl oz vegetable stock

750 ml/25 fl oz milk

1 large Bramley apple, grated (or other tart, cooking apple, if unavailable)

salt and freshly ground black pepper

METHOD

✳ Preheat the oven to 200°C/400°F.

✳ Toss the parsnips in half the olive oil and spread them out on a baking tray. Roast for 20 to 25 minutes until golden brown. Set aside.

✳ Heat the remaining olive oil and the butter in a large saucepan. Add the diced onion and curry paste and fry gently for 3–4 minutes. Then add the roasted parsnip, stock and milk. Bring to the boil, then reduce to a simmer and cook for a further 5 minutes, or until the parsnip is very soft.

✳ Add the grated apple and then blend until smooth using a stick blender or in a food processor. Season to taste with salt and pepper. Warm through gently before serving. Serve with Parsnip Chips.

PARSNIP CHIPS

Serves 4

INGREDIENTS

1 lb/450 g parsnips

4 tablespoons olive oil

sea salt and pepper

METHOD

✳ Preheat the oven to 190°C/375°F.

✳ Using a peeler or mandolin shave the parsnips into thin slices. Blot them on kitchen paper to remove any moisture, then lightly toss in olive oil and spread an even layer on one or two baking trays. Sprinkle generously with sea salt and black pepper. Roast in the oven for approx. 20–25 minutes, turning frequently, until golden at the edges—keep an eye on them since they may cook faster than this!

✳ Turn out onto kitchen paper to drain any excess oil—they should crisp up as they cool. Serve warm or cold.

ROASTED ROOT VEGETABLES TOSSED WITH WHOLE GARLIC CLOVES AND OREGANO

Serves 4

This is a quick, easy and lazy way to cook winter vegetables as it only uses one baking tray. However, it also produces the most delicious results—slightly crispy, slightly sweet, intense vegetables. Excellent served with any roast meat.

INGREDIENTS

1 head garlic
2 large carrots
2 large parsnips
½ medium celeriac
2 tablespoons olive oil
1 tablespoon dried oregano
salt

METHOD

❋ Preheat the oven to 190°C/375°F.

❋ Peel the garlic but leave the cloves whole. Peel the carrots and cut into finger length quarters. Peel the parsnips and celeriac and cut into pieces the same size as the carrots. Toss all the vegetables in a bowl with the olive oil, oregano and a good sprinkle of salt.

❋ Spread the vegetables on a baking tray in one flat layer and bake in the oven for 30 minutes. Turn the vegetables over and continue to bake for a further 20 minutes or until golden and crisp at the edges.

CARROT AND SESAME SALAD

Serves 4

This is simple, but good. The nutty flavour of the sesame contrasts nicely with the sweet softness of grated carrot.

INGREDIENTS

4 large carrots
wedge of lemon
2 tablespoons sesame seeds
½ tablespoon white wine vinegar
2 tablespoons sesame oil
1 teaspoon white sugar
pinch of salt

METHOD

❄ Peel and grate the carrots and squeeze the lemon juice over them to stop them from going brown.

❄ Put the sesame seeds in a dry, non-stick frying pan over a medium heat and cook until golden and fragrant. Set aside to cool, then add them to the carrots.

❄ Combine the vinegar, oil, sugar and salt in a glass jar, shake well and pour over the carrots. Toss, refrigerate and serve when ready.

CARROT, LENTIL, ORANGE AND CORIANDER SOUP

Serves 4

INGREDIENTS

200 g/7 oz red lentils
1 tablespoon olive oil
1 medium onion, finely chopped
400 g/14 oz carrots, grated
1litre/35 fl oz vegetable or chicken stock
2 handfuls coriander, roughly chopped
salt and pepper
1 orange, zest and juice
fresh coriander and plain yoghurt to serve

METHOD

❋ Rinse the lentils in a sieve under cold water.

❋ Put the olive oil in a large saucepan over a medium heat. Soften the onion—about 3 minutes—stirring frequently. Add the lentils, carrots and stock. Bring to a simmer. Cook for 10 minutes and then add the chopped coriander, salt and pepper.

❋ Using a zester, remove the skin of the orange and set aside. Add the juice of the orange to the saucepan. Leave the pan to simmer until the carrots and lentils are soft, about 40 minutes.

❋ Once the vegetables are soft, serve the soup with fresh coriander, a dollop of thick plain yoghurt, a little fine orange zest and a little freshly ground black pepper.

CARROT, CELERIAC, APPLE AND RAISIN SALAD

Serves 4

This is a simple coleslaw, but one that appeals to adults and children alike. My middle child demands that I prepare this salad to take to school for class suppers. The crunch of the apple with the soft sweetness of celeriac and carrots makes this salad close to summer comfort food.

INGREDIENTS

2 tablespoons plain yoghurt
2 tablespoons mayonnaise
dash of white wine vinegar
2 teaspoons white sugar
juice of half a lemon
pinch of salt
2 large carrots
½ medium celeriac
2 Granny Smith apples
170 g/6 oz raisins

METHOD

❋ First mix together the yoghurt, mayonnaise, vinegar, sugar, lemon juice and salt. Taste and adjust seasoning as needed. It should be quite sharp as the carrot, apple and raisins will add sweetness.

❋ Peel and grate the carrots and celeriac on the widest grater. Add to the dressing and toss so that they do not brown. Remove the core, then chop the apples, with skins, into medium dice. Add, with the raisins, and toss so that everything is covered. Refrigerated for up to 4 hours.

CHAPTER 6

GREENS: BROCCOLI, SPINACH, CABBAGE AND CAULIFLOWER

This slightly eclectic group of vegetables represents the core of winter staples. Reliably robust, they are also packed with health benefits. This is what your mother meant when she told you to eat your vegetables.

Growing tips: In the kitchen garden at Pashley Manor spinach is a favourite as it can be picked just minutes before being used in the café. A variety called Perpetual, which is in fact a chard that tastes like spinach, is sown directly into the ground in August. It can be cut and it sprouts again, ad infinitum, providing fresh greens right through the winter months. It's then planted again in early spring for summer leafing.

BROCCOLI, DRIED CRANBERRIES AND BACON SALAD

Serves 4

INGREDIENTS

1 large head broccoli
110 g/4 oz dried cranberries
6 rashers bacon
120 ml/4 fl oz olive oil
juice of half a lemon
1 tablespoon white wine vinegar
1 tablespoon honey
pinch of salt

METHOD

※ Cut the broccoli into small florets. Put a steamer saucepan of water on to boil and steam the florets for a very short time—just enough to soften them slightly, but so that they remain crisp—less than 3 minutes. Remove from the heat and refresh in cold running water. Set aside to drain.

※ In a frying pan cook the bacon. When crisp, chop into small pieces using kitchen scissors. Toss the bacon, any bacon fat, dried cranberries and broccoli in a bowl.

※ In a glass jar, mix the other ingredients and shake well. Dress the salad and toss well.

SPINACH AND KENTISH BLUE CHEESE QUICHE

Serves 6

For the pastry
230 g/8 oz plain flour
125 g/4 oz cold, unsalted butter
1 egg yolk

For the filling
knob of butter and a dash of olive oil
2 medium leeks, finely sliced

4 large handfuls spinach leaves
115 g/4 oz Kentish Blue cheese (or a different
   crumbly blue cheese)
2 whole eggs, 1 yolk
10 fl oz/285 ml heavy cream
2 tablespoons chopped chives
salt and pepper
nutmeg, freshly grated

METHOD

※ Preheat oven to 190°C/375°F.

※ Put the flour and butter in a food processor and pulse until it forms fine breadcrumbs. Then add the egg yolk, pulse again and bring the mixture together in a ball with your hand. If it's still too dry, add a tablespoon of cold water and mix again. Press into a 23 cm/9 in loose bottomed pie tin and chill for 30 minutes.

※ Prick the pastry with a fork then line it with parchment (baking) paper and fill with baking beans or rice. Bake for 15 minutes, then remove the baking beans and cook for a further 10 minutes or until slightly golden. Remove and set aside in a cool, dry place.

※ Heat the butter and olive oil and briefly sauté the leeks. Be careful to make sure they're not greasy.

※ Put the spinach in a colander and wilt by slowly pouring a kettle of hot water over it. Then rinse with cold water and squeeze out. The spinach should be softened. Chop up finely. Spread the chopped spinach, crumbled cheese and leeks across the bottom of the quiche base.

※ In a bowl, mix the eggs, cream, chives, salt, pepper and freshly ground nutmeg. Pour over the cheese and spinach and bake for approximately 40 minutes or until golden and set in the centre.

SPINACH ROULADE WITH CREAM CHEESE AND SMOKED SALMON

Serves 8

This is a winning dish in the café at Pashley Manor Gardens. It looks sophisticated, but is very easy to make and mouth-watering.

INGREDIENTS
225 g/8 oz cooked spinach, water squeezed out
6 eggs, separated
salt and pepper
ground nutmeg
2 tablespoons Parmesan cheese, grated

For the filling
225 g/8 oz cream cheese, softened
225 g/8 oz smoked salmon slices
small bunch of watercress
lemon slices

METHOD
✳ Preheat oven to 200°C/400°F.
✳ Line a rectangular cookie tray with non-stick parchment (baking paper).
✳ Squeeze as much water out of the spinach as you can. Mix the spinach, egg yolks and lots of salt, pepper and nutmeg. In a separate bowl, beat the egg whites to stiff peaks. Fold the egg whites carefully into the spinach, trying to keep as much air in them as possible.
✳ Spread the mixture out across the tin and sprinkle with the cheese. Bake for 15 minutes. Set aside to cool.
✳ Once cool, gently spread the roulade with the cream cheese and then lay the smoked salmon across the top. Roll it up from one short end and transfer to a serving plate. Decorate with watercress and lemon and slice to serve.

MUSHROOMS STUFFED WITH SPINACH, BOURSIN AND HERBS

Serves 4

INGREDIENTS

4 large field mushrooms

olive oil

170 g/6 oz Boursin cream cheese

4 large handfuls fresh spinach leaves, finely chopped

2 teaspoons grated lemon zest

1 garlic clove, minced

170 g/6 oz breadcrumbs

55 g/2 oz Parmesan cheese, grated

1 tablespoon chopped chives

1 tablespoon chopped parsley

METHOD

❋ Preheat the oven to 190°C/375°F.

❋ Clean and take the stems off your mushrooms. Place them on a baking tray and drizzle with olive oil and bake for 10 minutes, until some of the darker juices run off. Then, remove to a clean baking tray.

❋ Mix the cheese, shredded spinach, lemon zest and garlic. Fill the centre of each mushroom with the cream cheese and spinach mixture.

❋ Mix the breadcrumbs, Parmesan, chives and parsley. Sprinkle over the top of the mushrooms and bake until heated through, about 12 minutes.

SPINACH AND SMOKED HADDOCK GRATIN

Serves 4

As a child, smoked haddock was my favourite fish. In Canada, where I live now, it's hard to find, so it's a real treat to enjoy it when in England. The smoky fish flavour is the perfect foil for spinach and a creamy sauce. This is fabulously easy comfort food that works well for lunch with guests, or a weeknight supper. You can substitute smoked cod if you can't find haddock.

INGREDIENTS

450g/1 lb spinach
salt and pepper
450g/1 lb smoked haddock, skinned
200ml/7 fl oz crème fraîche (or double
  cream)
juice of ½ a lemon
55g/2 oz cheddar cheese, grated

25g/1 oz Parmesan cheese, grated
2 spring onions, sliced
nutmeg, grated

Topping

115 g/4 oz breadcrumbs
chopped parsley
25g/1 oz Parmesan cheese, grated

METHOD

※ Preheat oven to 160°C/320°F.

※ Wash the spinach in colander then wilt it by slowly pouring a kettle of hot water over it. Rinse again under a cold tap then squeeze out as much water as possible. You can do this by putting it in a clean tea towel and give it a twist to wring the moisture out. Roughly chop the spinach and season. Butter your baking dish—you can do one big family one, or individual ones. Scatter the chopped spinach evenly over the base.

※ Slice the fish into large chunks and put it on top of the spinach. Mix the crème fraîche, lemon juice, cheeses and nutmeg together and season well. Spread this mixture over the top of the fish and spinach. Top with the combined breadcrumbs, parsley and Parmesan and bake for approximately 30 minutes until it is bubbling and golden—perhaps a bit longer for a larger dish and a bit less for individual dishes.

STIR-FRIED CABBAGE
WITH GARLIC, BACON, CREAM AND NUTMEG

Serves 4

INGREDIENTS

4 rashers bacon

1 medium Hispi or Savoy cabbage, thinly sliced

dash of olive oil

3 cloves garlic, minced

170 ml /6 fl oz double cream

nutmeg, freshly grated

salt and pepper

METHOD

❋ Toss the bacon in a wok or deep frying pan. Cook until crisp, remove, drain any excess fat on a piece of absorbent paper and cut into small pieces using scissors. Set aside.

❋ Depending on how much fat the bacon has produced, you may need to add a slosh of olive oil to the pan. Do this, then add the cabbage and toss over a medium heat until it begins to wilt. Then add the garlic and continue to keep the cabbage moving in the pan until tinged with brown. Once the garlic is fragrant, add the bacon and the cream and turn the heat down to low. The idea is to heat the cream through but don't allow it to boil. Grate in plenty of fresh nutmeg, season and serve.

❋ This is particularly good served with roast pork.

CABBAGE SALAD WITH HOT BACON DRESSING

Serves 4

This is such a simple way to serve cabbage and a great winter starter instead of unseasonal summer leaves.

INGREDIENTS

medium Savoy cabbage, shredded

6 rashers thick bacon

olive oil

2 shallots, peeled and finely chopped

2 tablespoons dry white wine

2 tablespoons sherry vinegar

coarse sea salt and freshly ground black pepper

METHOD

※ Put the shredded cabbage in a salad bowl.

※ Cut the bacon into small pieces and put it in a frying pan over a medium-low heat. Slowly melt the fat from the bacon, removing it from the pan when it is crisp. Set aside on paper towel to drain and leave the fat in the pan.

※ You need about 5 tablespoons fat, so if there's obviously less than this, add a good slosh of olive oil, or more fat if you happen to keep some in your refrigerator. Then put the pan back on a medium heat and add the shallots, cooking until tinged brown at the edges. Add the wine and boil to burn off the alcohol, then the vinegar and briefly return it to a boil.

※ Remove the pan from the heat. Sprinkle the bacon bits over the cabbage, pour over the dressing, season, toss well and serve.

CLASSIC RED CABBAGE

Serves 4

Red cabbage is comfort food par excellence for me. It means it's the dead of winter, stew is in the offing and it's cold outside. It's also pretty and a welcome change in colour on the plate. You can throw more or less anything into red cabbage to make it your own, but I think a fruity zing is delicious. The important thing here is, don't add water, just cook very slowly!

INGREDIENTS
½ a red cabbage (they tend to be rather large), finely sliced
2 large red onions, finely sliced
4 Bramley apples (or other tart, cooking apples, if unavailable), cut into small chunks
120 ml/4 fl oz red wine vinegar
175 ml/6 fl oz orange juice
115 g/2 oz demerara sugar
115 g/4 oz raisins
zest of 1 orange
2 teaspoons ground cinnamon
1 cinnamon stick
2 star anise
salt and pepper

METHOD
❃ Mix all the ingredients in a large saucepan and put over a low heat. Slowly bring to a boil, reduce to simmer for at least one hour, or until the cabbage is soft. Remove the cinnamon stick and star anise.
❃ Red cabbage is usually the better the following day, once the flavours have had time to deepen.

ROASTED CAULIFLOWER AND STILTON SOUP

Serves 4

I don't like cauliflower unless it is roasted. When it is steamed or boiled, it is a pappy, white vegetable that can sometimes overpower other flavours. When it is roasted, it becomes nutty and mellow and a vegetable worth the space on the plate.

INGREDIENTS

1 medium head of cauliflower

3 tablespoons olive oil, plus a little extra

55 g/2 oz butter, plus a little extra

2 white onions, peeled and chopped

3 sticks of celery, roughly chopped

1 clove garlic

sprig of thyme

1.5 litres/50 fl oz vegetable or chicken stock

115 g/4oz Stilton cheese (or another creamy blue cheese, if unavailable)

60 g/2 oz pumpkin seeds

salt and pepper

METHOD

❊ Preheat the oven to 190°C/375°F.

❊ Cut the cauliflower into small florets. Set aside a large handful, enough to garnish the soup for serving. Toss the rest in a small amount of olive oil and spread out on a baking tray. Roast in the oven for 30 minutes, or until golden. Remove and set aside.

❊ In a large saucepan, melt the butter and oil, add the onions and soften, about 2 minutes. Add the celery and garlic, sweat over a medium-low heat for 5 minutes. Then add the sprig of thyme, roasted cauliflower and the stock. Bring to a boil and reduce to simmer for 15 minutes.

❊ Remove the thyme sprig. Using a stick blender or a food processor, pulse the soup until it's a smooth liquid. Return it to the saucepan over a low heat. Stir the Stilton cheese through the soup. Season to taste.

❊ In a dry frying pan, quickly toast the pumpkin seeds and set aside. Fry the remaining small pieces of cauliflower in a small amount of olive oil and butter, until crispy and browning at the edges.

❊ Serve the soup warm with pumpkin seeds and crispy cauliflower in the centre.

ROASTED CAULIFLOWER CHEESE WITH HAM, NUTMEG, MACE AND PARSLEY

Serves 4

INGREDIENTS

1 large head cauliflower
4 thick slices of ham or 8 thin ones
drizzle olive oil
salt

½ teaspoon ground mace
½ teaspoon freshly grated nutmeg
3 tablespoons chopped parsley
110 g/4 oz sharp cheddar, grated (optional,
    to add depth of flavour)

For the sauce

2 tablespoons butter
2 tablespoons plain flour
475 ml/16 fl oz milk
1 teaspoon salt

For topping

55 g/2 oz cheddar, grated
55 g/2 oz breadcrumbs
1 tablespoon chopped parsley

METHOD

❈ Preheat the oven to 190°C/375°F.

❈ Cut the cauliflower into medium florets. Spread them out across the bottom of a baking dish, drizzle with olive oil and a little salt. Bake for 30 minutes or until the cauliflower turns a golden brown at the edges.

❈ In a medium saucepan, melt the butter over medium-low heat. Add the flour and stir until smooth. Cook until the mixture turns a light, golden sandy colour, about 5 minutes.

❈ Meanwhile, heat the milk in a separate pan until just about to boil. Add the hot milk to the roux in a steady stream, whisking continuously until smooth. Bring to a boil, reduce to a simmer. Cook for 10 minutes, stirring constantly until sauce thickens, then remove from the heat. Season with salt, mace, nutmeg and stir in the parsley and a handful of the sharp, grated cheddar. Set aside in a warm place until ready to use.

❈ Remove the roasted cauliflower from the oven, cut the ham into smaller pieces and distribute around the dish. Cover with the cheesy white sauce and top with mixed grated cheese, parsley and breadcrumbs. Bake until bubbling and golden. Serve with plenty of green salad.

CHAPTER 7

LEAVES: ENDIVE, RADICCHIO, LAMB'S LETTUCE AND SALAD LEAVES

No lunch is complete without a pile of green and coloured salad leaves, so a wide variety of cut and come again leaves thrive in the walled kitchen garden at Pashley Manor. As lettuce becomes less appealing as summer ends, the crunch of Belgian endive, in both red and white varieties, offers an appealing salad alternative during the winter months.

Growing tips: Look for texture and colour when choosing your lettuce varieties. Cut and come again varieties mean you'll have lettuce all summer long. Try Lollo Rosso, Grenada, Edox and Lakeland, as well as the nutty flavour of Large Leaved lamb's lettuce for early spring salad leaves.

BELGIAN ENDIVE, ORANGE AND HAZELNUT SALAD

Serves 4

The pale, slightly bitter crunch of endive plays nicely with citrus and nuts. Since endive can be found year-round in most supermarkets, this is a good winter salad.

INGREDIENTS
4 Belgian endive
juice of ½ a lemon
2 oranges
115 g/4 oz whole hazelnuts
4 tablespoons olive oil
½ tablespoon white wine vinegar
pinch of sugar
pinch of salt

METHOD
* Slice the hard end off the endives then cut the remainder into pieces. Squeeze the lemon juice over it as you go so that it does not colour.
* Peel one of your oranges using a knife, removing all the pith as you go. Then, cut the orange pieces out in segments, between the pith dividers. Add to the endive. Squeeze the remaining orange over the endive for juice.
* Crush your hazelnuts into medium pieces using a mortar and pestle. Place them in a dry, non-stick frying pan and heat until they become slightly fragrant and toasted. Toss the majority of them through the salad, reserving some to decorate.
* Mix the olive oil, vinegar, sugar and salt in a glass jar and shake to combine. Dress the salad.

BELGIAN ENDIVE, APPLE, BLUE CHEESE AND WALNUT SALAD

Serves 4

This is a fabulous winter salad, served as a dinner party starter. Zinging with fresh crunch, it's a winner. Over the years I've used a combination of red skinned apples and white endive, but the best version includes white, red and green colours.

INGREDIENTS

large knob of butter
170 g/6 oz walnuts, chopped
2 teaspoons white sugar
4 white Belgian endive
2 red Belgian endive
2 Granny Smith apples
170 g/6 oz blue cheese (I use Stilton)

For the dressing

2 tablespoons olive oil
2 tablespoons walnut oil
1 tablespoon red wine vinegar
½ tablespoon white wine vinegar
1 teaspoon white sugar
salt and pepper

METHOD

- ❋ Melt the butter in a small pan. Add the walnuts and the sugar, toss until coated, glossy and slightly sticky. Set aside on paper towel.
- ❋ Chop your endives into matchsticks. Peel, core and cut the apple into matchsticks.
- ❋ Mix the dressing ingredients in a glass jar, shaking well to emulsify. Season to taste and add more sugar if it's too sharp for your taste.
- ❋ Combine the endive, apples, candied nuts and crumbled blue cheese. Cover with the dressing, toss and serve with walnut bread.

BELGIAN ENDIVE COOKED IN ORANGE JUICE WITH LEMON THYME

Serves 4

This is a delicious way to prepare endive—a tasty alternative to the usual rotation of winter vegetables.

INGREDIENTS
4 Belgian endives
250 ml/8 fl oz orange juice
2 tablespoons demerara sugar
zest of an orange
zest of a lemon
salt and pepper
small bunch of lemon thyme, leaves removed

METHOD
❋ Preheat oven to 190°C/375°F.
❋ Slice the endives lengthways, in half. Lay the halves side-by-side in a baking dish. Add the orange juice and sprinkle with the sugar, orange and lemon zest, salt, pepper and thyme leaves. Bake in the oven for 45 minutes.

MIXED SALAD LEAVES WITH GREEN APPLE, SOFT WHITE GOAT'S CHEESE, RAISINS, BACON AND A HONEY DRESSING

Serves 4

My youngest child calls this a chop-chop salad. It's her favourite summer holiday lunch and sometimes she freestyles, adding whatever she can find in the kitchen, which could include pine nuts, tomatoes and substituting the soft white goat's cheese with Parmesan, in large flakes.

INGREDIENTS

4 rashers thick bacon

2 tablespoons pumpkin seeds

½ large cucumber

115 g/4 oz soft white goat's cheese

2 Granny Smith apples

4 large handfuls of mixed lettuce leaves

115 g/4 oz raisins

For the dressing

4 tablespoons olive oil

1 tablespoon liquid honey

1 tablespoon white wine vinegar

1 teaspoon grainy mustard

METHOD

✳ Mix the dressing ingredients in a glass jar and shake well to emulsify.

✳ Cut the bacon into small pieces and gently fry it to render the fat and leave it crispy. Set aside on a piece of paper towel to drain.

✳ Toast the pumpkin seeds in the oven on a baking tray. Watch them carefully so that they do not burn.

✳ Slice the cucumber into medium dice. Using a fork, break the cheese into small lumps. Core the apples and cut them into medium dice.

✳ Gently tear the lettuce leaves into bite-sized pieces. Sprinkle them with the raisins, bacon pieces, cucumber, seeds and apple. Drizzle the dressing over the top to prevent the apple from colouring, then add the cheese to serve.

LAMB'S LETTUCE WITH CHICKEN LIVERS, BACON AND BALSAMIC DRIZZLE

Serves 4

There's something about the nutty juxtaposition of lamb's lettuce leaves with the creamy texture of chicken livers that makes this classic salad a winner as a light lunch or a dinner party starter. The important thing, however, is that the chicken livers shouldn't sit about once they come out of the pan.

INGREDIENTS
4 large handfuls of lamb's lettuce leaves
2 tablespoons pine nuts
4 thick rashers bacon
230 g/8 oz chicken livers, cleaned
55 g/2 oz butter
125 ml/4 fl oz balsamic vinegar
Maldon sea salt and freshly ground black pepper

METHOD
❊ Distribute your lamb's lettuce across four plates.
❊ Toast the pine nuts in a dry, non-stick frying pan. Set them aside. Chop the bacon into small pieces and add to a frying pan over a medium heat. Cook slowly to render the fat. Once cooked, remove to a piece of paper towel to drain and become crispy.
❊ Check the chicken livers and remove any pieces of membrane or green bits. Turn the heat to medium-high and add the butter to any bacon fat left in the pan. Toss in the chicken livers and keep them moving in the pan. Cook for approximately 3 minutes, or until slightly caramelised on the outside but still pink in the middle. Distribute across the lamb's lettuce leaves. Return the pan to the heat and de-glaze it with the balsamic vinegar. Drizzle the juices over each plate.
❊ Share the bacon bits out evenly, drizzle each salad with a little more olive oil, sprinkle with the pine nuts, a pinch of Maldon sea salt and a grind of fresh black pepper and serve immediately.

ITALIAN SALAD WITH PARMESAN, FIGS, PINE NUTS AND A HONEY DRESSING

Serves 4

In this salad the bitter crunch of the radicchio and curly endive leaves is offset by the sweet honey dressing, with pine nuts adding a smooth, nutty edge. In my opinion, it's the perfect mixture of sweetness and bitter flavours, rather like that other Italian export, the pre-dinner drink of Campari, orange juice and soda water.

For the dressing
4 tablespoons olive oil
1 tablespoon liquid honey
1 tablespoon white wine vinegar
1 teaspoon grainy mustard

For the salad
2 small heads radicchio
1 head of curly endive
115 g/4 oz pine nuts
230 g/8 oz Parmesan cheese, flaked
4 large figs

METHOD
✳ Mix the dressing ingredients in a glass jar and shake well to emulsify.
✳ Remove any unsightly leaves from the outside of the radicchio then tear the remaining leaves into small pieces. Choose the best of the curly endive and mix the two on four separate plates.
✳ In a dry frying pan, gently roast the pine nuts until golden brown and fragrant. Be very careful not to overcook them.
✳ Divide the Parmesan evenly between the plates. For the figs, if their skins are unblemished and clean, I like to leave them on. But if they are at all bruised or overripe (as tends to happen with figs), then peel them before cutting each one into four and distributing across the plates. Sprinkle each salad with pine nuts before drizzling with the honey dressing.

CHAPTER 8

BEANS, PEAS, ASPARAGUS AND BROAD BEANS

I really love this collection of green vegetables when each is at the peak of its respective season. There's no beating the inimitable vibrancy of asparagus, one of the harbingers of spring and all the good things to come from the garden. With the first asparagus, I salivate for sweet green peas or the crunch of various green beans, cooked in salads or eaten straight from the bush when picking. Even my dog loves raw green beans!

Growing tips: Tall towers of Firestorm and Moonlight Climbing Runner beans are festooned with red and white flowers come mid-late summer. These flowers are edible and look great on salads, but if you pick all the flowers to eat, you won't have any beans! Cobra variety climbing French beans are excellent for their long, elegant shape and crisp crunch, while Ferrari Dwarf French beans are compact and good for smaller gardens.

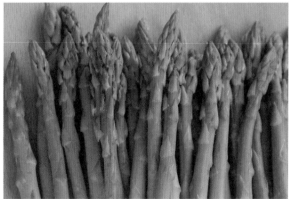

RUNNER BEANS WITH PARMESAN, OLIVE OIL AND LEMON

Serves 4

Nothing beats a runner bean eaten straight off the bush, but this simple way to prepare them comes a close second. An enormous pile of them is enough for a healthy, light summer lunch. Double the quantities in this recipe if you want enough for a whole lunch, rather than a side salad.

INGREDIENTS
450 g/1lb runner beans
4 tablespoons olive oil
juice of a lemon
115 g/4 oz Parmesan cheese, flaked
Maldon sea salt

METHOD
❊ Slice your beans at an angle to make bite sized, diamond shaped pieces. Place them in a steamer basket over a pan of briskly boiling water. Steam for about 3 minutes, or until al dente. They should squeak when you bite into them. Refresh the beans under cold water to stop further cooking.

❊ Toss the beans in the olive oil and lemon juice. Then, take a vegetable peeler and flake large pieces of wafer-thin Parmesan cheese on top of the beans. Sprinkle with Maldon sea salt flakes and serve.

PASHLEY CHICKEN WITH GREEN BEANS

Serves 4

This is a Pashley variation on that 1970s traditional favourite, Coronation chicken. This one, however, is a great way to incorporate lots of fresh vegetables and herbs from the garden.

INGREDIENTS

1 tablespoon mango chutney

1 tablespoon crème fraîche

1 tablespoon plain yoghurt

4 tablespoons mayonnaise

juice of ½ a lemon

1 teaspoon mild curry paste

½ a red pepper (capsicum), finely diced

2 sticks celery, finely diced

salt and black pepper

2 cooked smoked chicken breasts

115 g/4 oz French beans, cooked al dente

115 g/4 oz fresh peas, cooked al dente

1 tablespoon chopped parsley

1 tablespoon chopped chives

mango or orange slices to serve

METHOD

❋ Mix the mango chutney, crème fraîche, yoghurt, mayonnaise, lemon juice and curry paste in a bowl. Then add the red pepper pieces and celery. Season to taste.

❋ Remove any skin from the chicken breasts. Dice them into medium pieces and add to the sauce, which should coat it generously.

❋ Gently steam the beans and blanche the peas. Refresh them under cold running water, drain and add to the salad. Stir the chopped parsley and chives through the salad and serve with fresh mango or orange slices to decorate.

FRENCH BEAN AND BABY TOMATO SALAD

Serves 4

The beauty of this simple salad is in its colours. Vibrant red and deep green are a winning combination and it's an easy way to combine two vegetables that flourish in the garden at the same time of the season. If you grow orange tomatoes, you can throw these in too.

INGREDIENTS
230 g/8 oz French beans
230 g/8 oz small red tomatoes

For the dressing
4 tablespoons olive oil
½ tablespoon white wine vinegar
1 tablespoon red wine vinegar
1 tablespoon chopped chives
1 teaspoon white sugar
pinch of salt

METHOD
❋ Top and tail your French beans and cut them into pieces—thirds, depending on how long they are. Steam them over a pan of boiling water, until al dente. Immediately refresh them under cold running water. Set aside to drain.
❋ Cut your tomatoes in half and toss with the beans.
❋ Mix the ingredients for the dressing in a glass jar. Shake well to emulsify and pour over the tomatoes and beans before serving.

BROAD BEAN AND MINTED PEA SALAD

Serves 4

This vibrant, green coloured salad is delicious as a side salad, with fish (and chips!) or spread across small toasts as a pre-dinner amuse-bouche.

INGREDIENTS

230 g/8 oz fresh peas (you can also use frozen peas)
large handful fresh mint
250 ml/8 fl oz crème fraîche
230 g/8 oz broad beans
salt and pepper
4 rashers thick bacon

METHOD

❈ If your peas are frozen, allow them to defrost. Then put them into a food processor with the mint and whizz until they form a paste. Stir in the crème fraîche.

❈ Remove the broad beans from their pods. Drop the beans into a pan of boiling water for 2 minutes. Drain under cold water. Once the beans are cold, pop them from any leathery skins. Stir the broad beans through the pea and mint mixture. Season to taste.

❈ Cut the bacon into small pieces and cook slowly in a frying pan so that it renders its fat and becomes crispy. Remove from the pan and drain on a piece of paper towel.

❈ Serve as a side salad with bacon pieces on top, or on toasts with bacon to add a little crunch.

PEAS COOKED WITH FENNEL, LEEKS AND SHALLOTS

Serves 4

This is a really interesting medley of vegetables; delicious served with fish or lamb.

INGREDIENTS

1 medium head of fennel

large knob of butter

generous dash of olive oil

8 shallots, peeled and quartered

2 medium leeks, sliced

230 g/8 oz green peas

1 teaspoon sugar

handful chopped chives (optional)

squeeze of lemon juice

salt and pepper

METHOD

❊ Slice the fennel very thinly. Melt the butter and olive oil in a frying pan and add the fennel pieces. Sauté for 2 minutes over a medium heat. Then add the shallots. Cook for a further 2 minutes before adding the leeks. Keep the mixture moving in the pan, allowing it to turn slightly golden and caramelised. Finally, throw in the peas, sugar and chives and cook for a further minute. Remove from the heat, squeeze in lemon juice and season. Serve with white fish.

GREEN PEA AND MINT SOUP WITH BACON BITS

Serves 4

INGREDIENTS

2 medium onions
1 tablespoon olive oil
230 g/8 oz green peas
1 medium potato, peeled and diced
570 ml/20 fl oz chicken or veg stock
large handful mint leaves
salt and pepper
4 rashers bacon
175 ml/6 fl oz double cream

METHOD

✳ First, soften the onion in olive oil, then add the peas and potato. Cook for 5 minutes to soften, then add the stock and simmer for about 15 minutes. Transfer the soup to a food processor and pulse. You can leave this soup textured, or process until it is smooth. Add a small handful of mint leaves and pulse again. Season with salt and pepper.

✳ Fry the bacon until it has rendered its fat and is crispy. Chop into small pieces and set onto a piece of paper towel to drain. Sometimes I like to gently beat the cream so that it is lightly fluffy and float it across the top of the soup like a soft white cloud, scatted with bacon bits and chopped fresh mint, but you can also swirl it into the soup in liquid form.

PEA, RICE AND PRAWN SALAD
WITH LEMON DRESSING

Serves 4

This is another great salad that is perfect as a light lunch on its own, or served alongside other summer lunch treats such as the crab and leek tart in chapter 1.

INGREDIENTS

230 g/8 oz medium frozen cooked prawns

230 g/8 oz long grain or jasmine rice

230 g/8 oz frozen baby peas

115 g/4oz sugar snap peas

1 teaspoon sugar

230 g/8 oz cucumber, cut into medium chunks

6–8 spring onions, green parts removed, remainder chopped

large bunch of dill, chopped

extra dill sprigs and lemon to serve

For the dressing

4 tablespoons olive oil

1 teaspoon sea salt

juice of a lime

juice of half a lemon

1 dessertspoon white wine vinegar

2 teaspoons caster sugar

freshly ground black pepper

METHOD

❋ Put the prawns in colander to defrost.

❋ Cook the rice in salted water to al dente, drain and refresh under cold water. Allow it to drain through a colander for 10 minutes. Drop the frozen peas and the sugar snap peas into boiling water, to which you have added the teaspoon of sugar. Drain after about 45 seconds, refresh under cold water. Set aside to drain.

❋ Mix the rice, peas, spring onions and chopped dill.

❋ In a glass jar, mix the ingredients for the dressing and shake well to mix. Taste and adjust for more lemon juice or salt. Then toss the prawns in the dressing, before adding them and any extra dressing (drain the jar) to the rice and vegetables. Mix well.

❋ Serve decorated with dill sprigs and lemon.

ASPARAGUS SOUP WITH FLOATING TIPS

Serves 4

This gorgeous, velvety soup is one sure sign of early spring. It's most important to make this soup in two stages so that you get rid of any woody, fibrous bits of asparagus stalk.

INGREDIENTS

450 g/1 lb asparagus
2 litres/64 fl oz really good chicken stock
2 onions, chopped
dash of olive oil
knob of butter

1 large potato, diced
1 large carrot, finely diced
2 sticks celery, chopped
175 ml/6 fl oz cream
salt and freshly ground black pepper
freshly grated nutmeg plain yoghurt to serve

METHOD

※ First, cut off the asparagus tips and set them aside for serving.

※ Next, remove the woody white ends of the asparagus and discard. Cut the remaining asparagus into 2 cm long pieces. Put them in a saucepan and bring them to a simmer in the chicken stock. Simmer for 20 minutes or until soft.

※ Transfer the asparagus with the stock to a blender or food processor and pulse until pureed. Then using a medium sieve, push this asparagus-stock liquid through the sieve, discarding the fibrous bits left behind.

※ Soften the chopped onion in the olive oil and the butter over a medium heat. Add the diced potato, carrot, celery and sweat for a further 10 minutes. Next, add the asparagus-stock liquid. Simmer for 5 minutes—be careful not to overcook here or you will lose the vibrant asparagus flavour. Remove from the heat and put the soup in a food processor, or using a stick blender, puree the vegetable pieces until smooth. Add the cream. Season to taste with salt and pepper and fresh grated nutmeg.

※ In a small saucepan, blanche the asparagus tips in water or chicken stock. Drain and refresh under cold water.

※ Serve the soup with a dollop of plain yoghurt or a swirl of cream and floating asparagus tips.

CHAPTER 9

FENNEL AND AUBERGINES

Both of these vegetables are a staple in any Italian garden, and while they're easy to grow in almost any temperate climate, many cooks don't know what to do with their robust, distinct flavours in the kitchen. Here are just a few simple ideas.

Growing tips: Aubergines thrive in much the same environment as tomatoes, so plant them side-by-side. Fennel is a very versatile vegetable that is easy to grow and looks pretty in the garden. Try the Tauro F1 variety, with beautiful, dark green feathery fronds.

BAKED AUBERGINE IN FRESH TOMATO SAUCE

Serves 4

There's something about aubergines that screams out for the acidity of tomatoes. This is a simple gratin recipe that can be eaten as a main dish with a green salad.

INGREDIENTS

2 medium aubergines (eggplants)

2 tablespoons salt

1 quantity Fresh Plum Tomato Sauce (see page 70)

250 g/2 oz brown breadcrumbs

4 tablespoons chopped parsley

115 g/4 oz Parmesan cheese, freshly grated

freshly ground black pepper

METHOD

❋ Preheat oven to 190°C/375°F.

❋ Thinly slice the aubergine lengthways if it's a small one, or into rounds if it's a larger one. Put the pieces in a colander and sprinkle with salt. Set over the sink for at least 30 minutes. They should begin to drip.

❋ After 30 minutes, shake off any remaining salt, press the aubergines down to remove any final juice and pat dry with a clean tea towel.

❋ Line the bottom of a baking dish with half the tomato sauce. Layer the aubergines on top. Cover with remainder of tomato sauce. Season with pepper. Mix the breadcrumbs, parsley and two-thirds of the Parmesan. Distribute evenly over the top of the aubergines. Finish with the remaining cheese. Cover and bake for 40 minutes. Then remove the foil and allow to brown for a further 10 minutes.

❋ Serve with a green salad with a vibrant, slightly acid dressing.

AUBERGINE FRITTERS

Serves 4

While frying in oil doesn't feature much in my kitchen, it's worth it for these simple fritters, which are great pre-dinner snacks or even a light first course.

INGREDIENTS

2 medium aubergines (eggplants)

1 egg

2 tablespoons flour

2 tablespoons water

3 teaspoons ground cumin

plenty of salt and pepper

125 ml/4 fl oz sunflower oil

1 quantity Fresh Plum Tomato Sauce (see page 70)

METHOD

✳ Slice your aubergines into rounds about ½ cm thick.

✳ Mix the egg, water, flour (I use gluten free flour, or chickpea flour) and cumin. Season generously.

✳ Heat the sunflower oil over a medium heat in a frying pan. Once the oil begins to fizz in a lively manner (but do not let it smoke), dip the aubergine slices into the batter then place carefully into the pan. Cook until golden—about 2 minutes—then flip and cook for a further minute. Place on a piece of paper towel to drain any excess oil.

✳ Serve with warm, chunky fresh tomato sauce.

FENNEL WITH BUTTER AND LEMON THYME

Serves 4

INGREDIENTS

2 bulbs of fennel

115 g/4 oz butter

2 tablespoons olive oil

2 tablespoons lemon thyme, removed from stems and chopped a little

salt and pepper

juice of half a lemon

METHOD

❊ Remove any green parts, then thinly slice the fennel, obliquely (across the bulb at an angle).

❊ Heat the butter and oil in a deep frying pan over a medium heat and add the fennel. Cook and toss until softened, but not collapsing—about 6 minutes, depending on how thinly you have sliced it. Add the lemon thyme halfway through cooking. Season to taste with salt, pepper and lemon juice at the end of the cooking process.

FENNEL PUREE WITH CRÈME FRAÎCHE AND GRILLED FISH

Serves 4

INGREDIENTS

2 large bulbs of fennel
60 g/2 oz salted butter
125 ml/4 fl oz milk
175 ml/6 fl oz crème fraîche
freshly grated nutmeg
salt, pepper and lemon juice to taste

METHOD

❋ Remove the root and green tops of the fennel, leaving the central bulb. Finely slice.

❋ Melt the butter in a large frying pan over medium heat. Add the fennel and sauté for a couple of minutes. Then slowly add the milk and bring to a simmer until soft. This will add a creamy depth to the puree.

❋ Drain the fennel and pulse in a food processor until very smooth. Keep the milk to one side and use it to thin the puree if too thick. Discard any excess once you have stirred in the crème fraîche. There must be no stringy bits left at all. Gently stir in the crème fraîche, grate in the nutmeg, add salt, pepper and lemon juice to taste.

❋ Serve with grilled white fish.

FENNEL, ORANGE AND CHICKEN SALAD

Serves 4

INGREDIENTS

4 chicken breasts

2 tablespoons very finely chopped mixed fresh herbs

salt and fresh black pepper

knob of butter

3 tablespoons olive oil

125 ml/4 fl oz orange juice

zest and fruit of 2 oranges

3 tablespoons chopped parsley

2 bulbs of fennel

60 ml/2 fl oz sherry vinegar

METHOD

❋ Preheat the oven to 190°C/375°F.

❋ Roll the chicken breasts in salt, fresh black pepper and the mixed herbs. Heat the butter and a spoonful of olive oil in a frying pan and seal the chicken on all sides. Remove from the frying pan and bake, covered, in the oven for about 20 minutes, or until just cooked through.

❋ Cover the chicken and set it aside. Reserve the cooking juices and once cool, combine with the orange juice, half of the orange zest, half of the parsley, olive oil, sherry vinegar and check seasoning.

❋ Slice the fennel very finely, then toss it in the dressing. Cover the bottom of a serving dish or individual salad plates. Slice the chicken into thin slices and layer on top.

❋ Cut the orange away from the pith, slice into pieces across the orange and distribute across the salad. Cover with any remaining dressing, decorate with parsley and remaining orange zest.

CHAPTER 10

MID-SUMMER FRUIT: RASPBERRIES, GOOSEBERRIES, CHERRIES, BLACKBERRIES, RED, WHITE AND BLACK CURRANTS

A huge number of berries grow in the garden at Pashley Manor and they glisten, shiny and sticky, deep red, black and purple in the summer sun. They're a magnet to birds, so over the years a series of wrought iron berry cages has also grown in the garden to keep the birds out and the berries in.

Growing tips: As soon as a berry ripens, the birds will eat it before you can pick it. You must cover berries with bird-proof netting or wire if you're hoping for a decent harvest.

RASPBERRY AND HAZELNUT ROULADE

Serves 8

There's just something about the texture of hazelnuts, which grow in all the hedgerows in Kent and Sussex, and the tender softness of raspberries and meringue, that makes a perfect sweet finish to any meal. An added bonus is that both fresh raspberries and hazelnuts are available at the same time of year.

For the roulade
55 g/2 oz hazelnuts
3 large egg whites
175 g/6 oz caster sugar
½ teaspoon vanilla extract
½ teaspoon white wine vinegar
1 teaspoon corn flour

For the filling
250 ml/8 fl oz double cream
125 ml/4 fl oz full fat yoghurt
icing sugar
115 g/4 oz fresh raspberries
50 g/1.7 oz or ½ bar of 85% dark chocolate

METHOD

❉ Preheat oven to 190°C/375°F.

❉ Peel any papery skins off the hazelnuts. Crush them into small pieces using a mortar and pestle. Spread out on a baking sheet and roast in the oven until fragrant—just a few minutes. Keep an eye on them so that they don't burn. Set aside to cool.

❉ Line a baking sheet with greaseproof paper, making sure that it rises about an inch above all sides.

❉ Beat the egg whites to soft peaks and then slowly, but continuously, add the sugar and continue to beat. Once all the sugar has been combined, add the vanilla, then the white wine vinegar and corn flour until everything is well combined. Next fold in the hazelnuts.

❉ Spread the meringue mixture evenly over the tray and bake for 15 minutes. Remove and set aside to cool.

❉ Beat the cream and fold in the yoghurt, as well as a couple of spoonfuls of icing sugar. Carefully fold the raspberries into the cream mixture.

❉ Next, flip your meringue over onto a piece of greaseproof paper. Peel off the sheet on which it was baked. Spread the cream mixture over the exposed surface and using the paper, carefully roll up your roulade. Don't worry about cream oozing out, you can clean this up, or eat it, later!

❉ Gently melt the chocolate over a bain-marie and drizzle it over the top of the roulade. Decorate with extra raspberries, mint leaves and powdered sugar.

GOOSEBERRY FOOL WITH GOOSEBERRY AND ELDERFLOWER JELLY

Serves 6

One day recently, my mother appeared in the kitchen holding a large basket of gooseberries. A couple of hours later, she'd produced this delicious pudding, pairing a creamy gooseberry fool with the sparkling texture of an elderflower jelly, with gooseberries suspended like balloons in a summer sky. It's a dinner party winner.

Gooseberry and Elderflower Jelly

350 g/12 oz green gooseberries

100 g/3.5 oz caster sugar

2 x 11 g sachets powdered gelatine

2 tablespoons elderflower cordial

350 ml/12 fl oz sparkling elderflower or sparkling wine

6 small silicone or dariole moulds (Silicone work best, but if you are using dariole moulds, just gently warm them in a sink of warm water before turning out the jellies.)

METHOD

❋ Top and tail the gooseberries, sprinkle the sugar over them, put them in saucepan with a lid and cook, gently, until just soft.

❋ In a separate bowl, add the gelatine to 3 tablespoons of water. Once the gooseberries are just soft, remove them from the heat and stir in the gelatine mixture—very gently so as not to break the fruit—then pour the whole lot into a bowl and leave to cool.

❋ As it cools and then becomes cold it will begin to turn syrupy (about 45–60 minutes), and at this stage pour in the elderflower cordial and the sparkling elderflower. Mix thoroughly, but gently, and then pour the jelly into individual moulds. Cover them with plastic wrap and chill in the refrigerator until needed.

Recipe continues on page 219

Gooseberry Fool

900 g/2 lb green gooseberries
2 tablespoons elderflower cordial
zest of an orange
55 g/2 oz demerara sugar
250 ml/8 fl oz full fat plain yoghurt
250 ml/8 fl oz cream, beaten

METHOD

※ Top and tail the gooseberries to remove any hard bits. Put them into a saucepan over a gentle heat with the elderflower cordial, orange zest and sugar. Cook until they collapse and go soft.

※ Separate the berries from the juice, setting the juice aside. Using a hand blender or food processor, pulse until they form a puree. Then press through a sieve to remove any seeds and add back in any juice needed to make a puree the consistency of apple sauce.

※ Combine the yoghurt and cream then fold through the gooseberry puree and taste for sweetness. Adjust according to taste.

※ Serve alongside the gooseberry jellies.

GINGER AND GOOSEBERRY CUSTARD TART WITH VANILLA AND ELDERFLOWER

Serves 8

For the crust

230 g/8 oz gingernut biscuits

115 g/4 oz butter

30 g/1 oz demerara sugar

For the filling

approx. 20 gooseberries

4 egg yolks

175 ml/6 fl oz double cream

55 g/2 oz sugar

2 tablespoons elderflower cordial

½ teaspoon vanilla extract

½ teaspoon vanilla bean paste

175 ml/6 fl oz double cream

METHOD

❊ Preheat oven to 190°C/375°F.

❊ Put your gingernut biscuits in a plastic bag and bash it until you have crumbs, or whizz the biscuits in a food processor. Melt the butter and add it, with the sugar to the crushed biscuits. Stir well and press the biscuits into the base of a 23 cm/9 in loose-bottomed pie tin. Bake for about 10 minutes then remove from the oven.

❊ Turn the oven up to 200°C/400°F. Top and tail the gooseberries to remove any hard black bits. To make the custard, mix the remaining ingredients in a bowl. Distribute the gooseberries across the biscuit base. Pour the custard on top. Bake for 35 to 40 minutes or until the custard has set and turned golden and the gooseberries are soft.

❊ Decorate with icing sugar.

BLACKBERRY TARTS WITH ROSEWATER CREAM

Makes one 23 cm/9 in tart shell, four small ones

These look so pretty and are easy to prepare, making the best of hedgerow blackberries, found all over the English countryside in late summer and early autumn. But it's the secret ingredient that gives these little tarts the wow! factor.

For the pastry
120 g/4 oz unsalted butter, room temperature
45 g/1.5 oz icing sugar
1 large egg yolk
115 g/4 oz all-purpose flour
½ teaspoon salt
1 tablespoon cream or milk, if needed

For the filling
175 ml/6 fl oz thick cream, whipped
175 ml/6 fl oz plain yoghurt
2 tablespoons icing sugar
2 tablespoons rosewater
230 g/8 oz blackberries
mint leaves and icing sugar to serve

METHOD

※ The trick to making successful pâte sucrée is to have the butter at the right temperature and not to overwork the dough.

※ Beat the butter and sugar together until creamy. Add the egg yolk. Scrape down the sides of your bowl. With the mixer on low, add the flour and salt until the mixture comes together. If it is too dry and remains crumbly, add a tiny bit of cream or milk.

※ Wrap the pastry in plastic wrap and chill for at least an hour, or for up to two days.

※ When you are ready to make your tarts, allow the pastry to warm slightly on the counter or it will be too hard to roll out. It should still be cool to the touch.

※ When you are ready, roll out the dough between two sheets of non-stick parchment. Roll it out as thin as you dare—these shells are best if they are like shortbread wisps. Using a small plate, or any round slightly bigger than your tart tins, cut out circles. Lay the pastry into the baking tins and make the top edges neat with a knife. Stick any holes together using extra pastry as a patch. Refrigerate for a further 30 minutes.

※ Prick the shells with a fork and line them with parchment and rice or baking beans. Bake for about 20 minutes, then remove the paper and baking beans and cook for a further 5 to 7 minutes, until golden.

※ For the filling, combine the whipped cream and yoghurt, icing sugar and rosewater in a bowl. Fill the centre of each tart with this mixture, top with blackberries and decorate with tiny sprigs of mint and icing sugar.

※ Serve immediately, before the pastry has time to go soft.

BLACKBERRY AND APPLE MERINGUE

Serves 6

This is my girls' favourite pudding. They shriek with joy when the slightly browned, puffy cloud of meringue emerges from the oven. Then they lather it with thick cream. Not for the faint of heart, but a good winter warmer as the apple compote and blackberries can both be frozen when in season.

INGREDIENTS

4 apples, not Granny Smith (sweeter, softer apples work better here)
125 ml/4 fl oz orange juice
2 teaspoons cinnamon
½ teaspoon ground cloves
4 tablespoons demerara sugar
squeeze of lemon juice
170 g/6 oz blackberries
1 tablespoon elderflower cordial

For the meringue

3 large egg whites
175 g/6 oz caster sugar
½ teaspoon vanilla extract

METHOD

❊ Preheat oven to 175°C/350°F. Peel, core and roughly chop the apples. Put them in a saucepan with the orange juice, cinnamon, ground cloves and 2 tablespoons of the sugar. Cover and bring to a simmer. Cook until the apples are soft. Mash them with a fork.

❊ Toss the blackberries in the elderflower cordial, lemon juice and remaining sugar. Mix them into the apples. Fill a deep-sided baking dish with the fruit.

❊ For the meringue, beat the egg whites to soft peaks. Turn the beater down to low and slowly, but continuously add the sugar, then the vanilla.

❊ Cover the top of the fruit mixture with mounds of pillowy meringue. Bake for 35 minutes, or until golden on top. Serve with plenty of thick cream.

CHERRIES COOKED IN RED WINE

Serves 4

The cherry season is so short that this simple recipe is a great way to preserve this early-season fruit so that you can enjoy them year-round. Once cooked, they freeze well.

INGREDIENTS

900 g/2 lb cherries, preferably morello and local black
juice of 2 oranges, zest of one of them
115 g/4 oz demerara sugar
250 ml/8 fl oz red wine
2 cinnamon sticks

METHOD

✳ Remove the stones from the cherries. This is a tiresome and messy job, but really worth doing.
✳ Put the pitted cherries in a saucepan with the orange juice, zest, sugar, red wine and cinnamon sticks. Bring very slowly to a simmer and cook until soft, but not soggy. About 10 minutes. Adjust sugar to taste.
✳ Serve with thick double cream or ice cream or freeze in a plastic container with the juice.

CHERRY BRANDY

Makes 1.5 litres/3 pints

My mother makes cherry brandy in demijohn jars. They are huge—several litres. I think you need to find a 2-litre bottle or some smaller preserving jar, unless you really, really love drinking cherry brandy.

INGREDIENTS
450 g/1 lb cherries, ⅔ morello and ⅓ sweet cherries, or all morello
a couple of drops of almond essence
1 bottle brandy
approx. 225 g/8 oz sugar

METHOD
❋ Remove the pits from a large handful of cherries. Crush the stones. Put the whole cherries, pitted cherries and stones in your chosen glass bottle or jar. Add the almond essence, brandy and sugar.

❋ Give the jar a good shake and set it aside in a dark place for at least six months, or up to three years. It just gets fruitier the longer you leave it.

❋ When you are ready to decant your cherry brandy, pass the liquid through a sieve, then through a coffee filter into sterilised, pretty bottles.

❋ You can keep the pitted cherries, cook with a small amount of orange juice, and serve with meringues and ice cream.

MIXED BERRY COMPOTE

Serves 4

While this may appear to be simply cooked summer fruit, making a really good compote—perfect for breakfast or pudding—is a bit more fiddly than you might imagine. The velvety smooth, lustrous fruit in a rich, red juice is worth the effort.

INGREDIENTS

55 g/2 oz red currants
55 g/2 oz black currants
55 g/2 oz white currants
juice and zest of 1 orange
60 ml/2 fl oz elderflower cordial
55 g/2 oz caster sugar
115 g/4 oz black cherries
115 g/4 oz morello cherries
125 ml/4 fl oz orange juice
55 g/2 oz caster sugar
60 ml/2 fl oz elderflower cordial
115 g/4 oz blueberries
115 g/4 oz blackberries or loganberries
115 g/4 oz raspberries
extra sugar, lemon or lime juice to taste

METHOD

❋ Put the currants (any mixture of colours you like) into a saucepan with the orange juice, zest, elderflower and sugar. Gently bring to the boil and simmer for 10 minutes. Then press the currants through a sieve, reserving the thick puree.

❋ Add the cherries to the orange juice, sugar and elderflower cordial. Bring to a simmer and poach until soft—a few minutes. Add the blueberries and blackberries or loganberries (or any solid berry fruit) and return to a simmer. Then turn off the heat. Finally, add the raspberries. The residual warmth will cook them through without breaking them up.

❋ Add the currant puree to the other fruit and stir very gently. Taste and adjust by adding more sugar, or lemon or lime juice for acidity.

MIXED BERRY TERRINE

Serves 6, makes one 450 g/1 lb loaf pan

INGREDIENTS

450 g/1 lb mixed soft fruit (blueberries, currants, raspberries, strawberries)
55 g/2 oz caster sugar
1 store-bought Madeira cake
mint leaves to decorate

METHOD

❋ Hull the strawberries and if they are large, cut them into smaller pieces so that they're about the same size as the other fruit you have chosen. Gently mix the sugar into the fruit, and add a couple of spoons of water. Put the fruit in a saucepan over a low heat. Slowly allow the fruit to cook and release its juices. Once it has come to a simmer, turn off the heat and set aside.

❋ Slice your Madeira cake into pieces that are a couple of centimetres wide. Line the inside of the loaf tin you are using with plastic wrap, then a layer of cake across the bottom of the tin, trimming where necessary. Then add about half the berries, then another layer of cake, then more berries, finishing with a layer of cake. Fold the plastic wrap over. Next, find something heavy like a couple of cans of baked beans or an unopened bag of flour and put it on the terrine to compress it.

❋ Set aside in the fridge for at least 2 hours before serving.

❋ When you are ready to serve it, remove the heavy objects, unfold the plastic wrap and put a large serving plate over the bottom of the terrine. Flip the plate. Remove the plastic wrap. Decorate with fresh berries and some mint.

❋ Slice and serve with any leftover cooked berries and cream.

MIXED BERRY TRIFLE

Serves 4

INGREDIENTS
For the crème anglaise custard
250 ml/8 fl oz heavy cream
1 teaspoon vanilla bean paste
5 egg yolks
65 g/2.2 oz caster sugar

4 slices leftover Mixed Berry Terrine
125 ml/4 fl oz thick cream, whipped
fresh berries and mint to decorate

METHOD
* In a small saucepan, heat the cream and vanilla bean paste until just bubbling.
* In a separate bowl, whisk together the egg yolks and sugar until pale. Then pour half a cup of hot milk onto the egg yolks. Incorporate and then pour this mixture slowly back into the remaining hot milk, stirring with a whisk all the time. Keep the custard over a low heat and stir until the sauce begins to thicken and coats the back of a spoon with a thick layer. Set aside to cool.
* When you are ready to assemble your trifle, break up the slice of terrine in the bottom of a serving glass, spoon the crème anglaise on top and follow with a large dollop of whipped cream. Decorate with fresh berries and a sprig of mint.

BLUEBERRY CHEESECAKE

Serves 8

This very simple cheesecake looks beautiful and is a favourite in the café in the gardens at Pashley. You don't have to bake the base, but I think it adds to the chewy texture, which is nice.

For the crust
8 oz/230 g gingernut biscuits
115 g/4 oz butter
30g/1 oz demerara sugar

For the filling
55 g/2 oz icing sugar
1 tablespoon honey

230 g/8 oz plain cream cheese, room temperature
175 ml/6 fl oz cream
175 g/6 oz blueberries
1 heaped teaspoon gelatine (you can also use agar-agar)
115 g/4 oz crab apple or quince or red currant jelly

METHOD

✳ Preheat oven to 190°C/375°F.

✳ Put your gingernut biscuits in a plastic bag and bash it until you have crumbs, or whizz the biscuits in a food processor. Melt the butter and add it, with the sugar, to the crushed biscuits. Stir well and press the biscuits into the base of a 23 cm/9 in loose-bottomed pie tin. Bake for about 10 minutes. Set aside to cool.

✳ Stir the icing sugar and the honey into the soft cream cheese. Then beat the cream and incorporate this too.

✳ Separate about half of the blueberries and squeeze a few in your fingers. Leave others whole. Then incorporate these into the cream cheese mixture. You might need to use your hands to do this.

✳ Fill the cooled ginger biscuit pie shell with the blueberry cream cheese mixture. Cover the surface with blueberries in a pretty pattern. Put it in the fridge to cool for at least 2 hours.

✳ Once cool and firm, melt the gelatine in whichever jelly you are using in a saucepan over low heat until just dissolved. Once it has melted, set aside until it begins to thicken slightly.

✳ Now, work quickly. Remove the blueberry cheesecake from the fridge and pour the jelly glaze over the top. Return to the fridge to set.

✳ Serve with Poached Blueberries with Rosewater.

POACHED BLUEBERRIES WITH ROSEWATER

Serves 4

INGREDIENTS
450 g/1 lb fresh blueberries
juice and zest of 1 orange
55 g/2 oz demerara sugar
2 tablespoons rose flower water

METHOD
❊ Blueberries cook very easily, so be careful. Put all the ingredients in a small saucepan and slowly bring to a simmer. After 2 minutes turn off the pan. Taste for sweetness and acidity—you may need to add a squeeze of lime juice.

❊ Serve with the Blueberry Cheesecake.

CHAPTER 11

LATE-SEASON FRUIT: APPLES, PEARS, PLUMS, FIGS AND SLOES

There's something very comforting about late season fruit. The excitement of high-summer berries, the explosive taste of that first strawberry or the crunch and juice of a really good cherry has passed. Late season fruits last longer in your pantry, which makes them more versatile. These fruit conjure memories of mellow autumn Sunday lunches.

Growing tips: If you have a garden wall or fence, it's a great place to grow espaliered apples, pears and figs. While it's tricky to train the branches to grow along the flat surface at the outset, once you've tamed your tree, you'll find that it takes up much less space and produces far more fruit than its counterpart, allowed to grow in a conventional shape.

AUTUMN APPLE AND RAISIN CAKE

Makes one 900 g/2 lb loaf pan or two 450 g/1 lb loaf pans

namon flavours. The best thing about it is that you really don't have to be any good at making cakes—you can't fail with this one.

INGREDIENTS
170 g/6 oz butter
340 g/12 oz self-raising flour
2 teaspoons ground cinnamon
285 g/10 oz demerara sugar
85 g/3 oz raisins
2 eggs
250 ml/8 fl oz milk
450 g/1 lb grated apples

METHOD
❋ Preheat oven to 175°C/350°F.
❋ Melt the butter in a small saucepan. Mix in all the remaining ingredients, sifting in the flour and the spice. Pour into greased loaf tin or tins and bake for 1–1 ½ hours. The cake is cooked when it is chestnut brown on top and a skewer to the middle comes out clean.

PASHLEY APPLE CHUTNEY

Makes two 1-litre jars

This apple chutney is a signature flavour from my childhood table. Every year I make upwards of 30 jars of this chutney with apples that fall from the tree directly outside my kitchen window. My mother and the team at Pashley Manor make it in huge quantities for the restaurant in the garden and all the guests who pass through the house. It's a winner with cheese, quiche, pork pies, sausages and cold cuts.

INGREDIENTS
900 g/2 lb chopped apples
375 ml/12 fl oz apple cider vinegar
2 small onions, roughly chopped
230 g/8 oz raisins
230 g/8 oz brown sugar
3 teaspoons ground ginger
1 teaspoon ground cloves
1 teaspoon Jamaican allspice
2 teaspoons ground cinnamon

METHOD
❋ Peel, core and then roughly chop the apples. Put them in a deep saucepan with all the other ingredients and put over a very low heat with a lid. This needs to come very slowly to a low simmer. Don't be tempted to turn the heat up under this chutney or it will burn in no time.

❋ Simmer for 2 hours minimum, but anywhere up to 4 will be fine, the consistency just getting darker and stickier the longer you cook it. Stir anytime you remember or pass by the saucepan.

❋ Heat your jars in a warm oven (until they are too hot to hold). Pour the hot chutney into hot jars and seal immediately.

CLASSIC BAKED APPLES

Serves 4

This is a regular winter Sunday lunchtime pudding around our kitchen table. Deeply comforting, it's warming food for the winter months. It's also very convenient because you can prepare the apples a day in advance and store them somewhere cool. Just slide them into the oven an hour before you'd like to enjoy them.

INGREDIENTS

4 large Bramley apples (or other large, tart, cooking apples, if unavailable)
55 g/2 oz raisins
grated zest of one orange
grated zest of one lemon
2 teaspoons cinnamon
2 teaspoons ground cloves
2 tablespoons soft brown sugar
4 teaspoons marmalade
250 ml/8 fl oz orange juice

METHOD

✳ Preheat oven to 175°C/350°F.
✳ Carefully remove the core of each apple, but do not puncture right through. Try to leave one end intact to keep any juice inside.
✳ Then, using a sharp knife, score the skin around the middle of the apple, so that it does not split while cooking.
✳ Mix the raisins with the lemon and orange zest, half the cinnamon, cloves and sugar. Put a teaspoon of marmalade in the bottom of each apple, then stuff the hole in the apple with the raisin mixture.
✳ Put the apples in a baking dish, mix the remaining cinnamon, cloves and sugar with the orange juice and pour it around them. Sprinkle with any remaining raisin mixture.
✳ Cook for an hour, or until turning golden brown on top. Serve with the sticky sauce and plenty of thick cream or ice cream.

PLUMS STEWED WITH VANILLA

Serves 4

There is a plum tree in the garden that rains plums come August. When I was young, my mother could not pick them, nor gather them from the ground, fast enough, so a delicious, sweet and sticky plum mess would form. The wasps loved them, but so did we, cooked with vanilla. The thing about plums is that the vanilla brings out the sweetness. There's no need to add extra sugar unless they are really under ripe.

INGREDIENTS
900 g/2 lb ripe plums
4 vanilla pods
2 cinnamon sticks
1 teaspoon ground cinnamon
500 ml/16 fl oz orange or apple juice

METHOD
❋ Halve the plums and remove the stones. Add them, with all the other ingredients, to a saucepan. Bring to a slow simmer over a low heat. Cook until just soft—less than 10 minutes—you do not want them to dissolve.
❋ Serve with vanilla ice cream or thick, double cream.
❋ You can then use any leftovers the following day to make a fool. Put a few plums in the bottom of a tall glass. Using a hand blender, puree the remainder and combine with crème fraîche. Layer this on top of the cooked plums. Decorate with a vanilla pod and a sprinkle of crunchy sugar.

PLUM TART WITH A GINGER CRUST

Serves 8

In my early twenties, I lived in Paris. My boyfriend's mother owned a very chic shop that sold exquisite French tartes to the good ladies of the 7th arrondissement. The crusts were chewy and slightly caramelised, crunchy and mouth-watering, the inside filled with decadent custard and sticky fruit. I think this plum tart would do Tarte Julie proud.

For the crust
230 g/8 oz gingernut biscuits
115 g/4 oz butter
27 g/1 oz demerara sugar

For the filling
10 plums
4 egg yolks
55 g/2 oz sugar
½ teaspoon vanilla extract
½ teaspoon vanilla bean paste
1 teaspoon cinnamon
175 ml/6 fl oz double cream

METHOD
❋ Preheat oven to 190°C/375°F.
❋ Put your gingernut biscuits in a plastic bag and bash it until you have crumbs, or whizz the biscuits in a food processor. Melt the butter and add, along with the sugar to the crushed biscuits. Stir well and press the biscuits into the base of a 23 cm/9 in loose-bottomed pie tin. Bake for about 10 minutes.
❋ Halve your plums and remove the stones. Mix the remaining ingredients in a bowl. Pour into the biscuit base, then distribute the plums across the top. Bake for 30 minutes or until golden brown on top.
❋ Decorate with icing sugar.

PLUM SLICES

Serves 9

With thanks to Sian Gilchrist for this delicious recipe for plum slices which are irresistible at any time of day, as a snack, or pudding with cream or custard. Sian suggests that they can also be made with apples, pears, damsons, apricots and almonds, figs and walnuts.

INGREDIENTS

450 g/1 lb fresh plums, halved, stoned and sliced
2 teaspoons cinnamon
350 g/12 oz plain flour
175 g/6 oz porridge oats
1 teaspoon salt
1 teaspoon mixed spice
285 g/10 oz butter
140 g/5 oz soft brown sugar

METHOD

✳ Preheat the oven to 180°C/355°F.
✳ Toss the plums in half of the cinnamon.
✳ Mix the flour, oats, salt, mixed spice and remaining cinnamon in a bowl. Melt the butter with the sugar in a small pan. Pour this over the oat mixture. Mix well. Press half of the mixture into the bottom of a small, parchment lined baking tray. Layer the plums on top of the oats and cover with remaining oat mixture. Press down.
✳ Bake for 30 minutes. Allow to cool in the tin before serving.

PEARS COOKED IN WINE, CINNAMON AND BROWN SUGAR

Serves 4

This is such a pretty pudding and so easy. It's perfect dinner party fare when served with ice cream, as you can prepare it well in advance and just add the ice cream at the last minute.

INGREDIENTS

4 elegant pears, slightly under ripe (I choose for shape)

500 ml/16 fl oz wine—it could be red, white or even port

55 g/2 oz soft brown sugar

2 vanilla pods

2 cinnamon sticks

1 teaspoon ground cinnamon

METHOD

※ Carefully peel the pears, leaving the stalk intact. Place them in a saucepan, lying down, but without too much extra room, or the liquid will not be enough.

※ Add the wine. Red or port will turn your pears a deep, rich red colour on the outside, paler when you cut into them, while white wine will leave them golden. Add the sugar, vanilla and both kinds of cinnamon.

※ Bring the saucepan to a very slow simmer. Cook for about 30 minutes, turning carefully once, so that both sides come into contact with the cooking liquid.

※ Taste for sweetness and if needed, add more sugar. Remove the pears and the vanilla pods and cinnamon sticks from the cooking liquid and set aside. Then turn up the heat under the liquid and reduce it by one third, until it becomes more viscous and sticky.

※ Using a sharp knife, slit open the vanilla pods and scrape out the seeds. Add them to the liquid. Turn off the heat and return the pears to the saucepan until you are ready to serve.

※ Serve with vanilla ice cream and decorate with the cinnamon sticks.

GRILLED FIGS

Serves 4

While beautiful, the fig tree in the garden is a pretty hit and miss affair. Some years there is great bounty, others it produces just one or two fruit, which makes them all the more delicious and precious. When there's bounty, this is an easy, but good thing to do with figs. It applies to peaches too.

INGREDIENTS
4 large figs
pinch of cinnamon
2 tablespoons caster sugar
drizzle of balsamic vinegar

METHOD
✳ Cut the figs in half. Place them, cut side up, on a tray covered in foil. Sprinkle with cinnamon and sugar. Place them under the grill until the sugar starts to bubble and caramelise—keep a sharp eye on them so that they do not burn.
✳ Remove from the oven, serve with ice cream and a drizzle of aged, thick balsamic vinegar, or with soft, white goat's cheese and a curl of prosciutto.

SLOE GIN

Makes approximately 2 litres/3.5 pints

The real end of autumn, that marker that defines the end of golden days and blowing leaves, is the first hard frost. It also means that parsnips and leeks will soon be ready for harvest, and in the wild it means that sloes are ready for picking.

I suggest you find a 2-litre glass bottle for making this quantity of sloe gin. You can scale up this recipe if you plan to make it in huge demijohn bottles, as my mother does.

INGREDIENTS

approx. 450 g/1 lb sloes
1 750 ml/26 fl oz bottle gin
approx. 175 ml/6 fl oz brandy
230 g/8 oz sugar
a few drops of almond essence

METHOD

❋ Pick over the sloes to remove leaves and stems and if you have picked them before a couple of good hard frosts, put them in a plastic bag in the freezer for at least 24 hours. Prick them with a fork.

❋ Put the sloes and all the other ingredients into your bottle. If there's a large amount of empty space, top up with more gin. Seal well. Shake well, at least three times a week. Store in a cool, dark place for at least six months, or longer, as you like. My mother sometimes leaves it for up to three years. The longer you leave it, the fruitier it will become. Sweetness depends on how much natural sugar there was in the fruit at the time of picking. You can adjust this by blending different vintages or by adding a small amount of sugar melted in brandy at the time of bottling.

❋ When you are ready to decant the sloe gin, drain it through a sieve and discard the sloes. Then drain it again through paper coffee filters until all debris has been removed and you are left with a dark purple liquid.

CHAPTER 12

RHUBARB, JAMS AND JELLIES

The arrival of the first pale pink stalks of rhubarb in my kitchen is another moment of great joy, a signal that winter is almost behind us. My children hop with glee when the first bowl of warm rhubarb compote with thick cream lands on the table in front of them.

Growing tips: Once established, rhubarb is easy to grow and provides stalks throughout the spring and summer. It does take up rather a lot of space however, with its large leaves. The secret to the soft, pale pink, early spring stalks is to deprive them of light. When you notice the first shoots in spring, cover the rhubarb with a tall pot with a hole in the top (it can be a piece of wide drainage pipe) to allow water and a small amount of light to penetrate. This will encourage the rhubarb to grow towards the light. It's stressful for the plant, so generally the pots are removed by late spring.

RHUBARB POACHED IN ORANGE FLOWER WATER

Serves 4

This is an early season winner. When asparagus is bringing much welcome green to our plates, rhubarb provides fresh, tart fruity occasions for celebration at the other end of the meal.

INGREDIENTS

8 sticks of rhubarb, as pale as possible
zest and juice of 1 orange
top up with more orange juice to make approx. 125 ml/4 fl oz
115 g/4 oz demerara sugar
½ teaspoon ground cinnamon
1 cinnamon stick
3 tablespoons orange flower water

METHOD

❋ Slice the rhubarb into 2–3 cm (1 in) lengths. Put them in a saucepan with the juice, zest, sugar, cinnamon and orange flower water. Slowly, bring the pan to a simmer. Cook for a very short time—less than 5 minutes. Remove from the heat and set aside to cool. You want the rhubarb to be soft, but not fall apart. It's a delicate balance and you must watch it like a hawk.

❋ Serve warm or cold with a generous puddle of thick cream.

❋ My mother makes this with fresh ginger instead of orange flower water. Replace the orange flower water with about four thin slices of fresh, peeled ginger. Remove the ginger and cinnamon stick before serving.

RHUBARB FOOL WITH GINGER COOKIES

Serves 4

This is an easy pudding—quick to prepare and decadently creamy. Thanks to Sian Gilchrist for this recipe.

Rhubarb fool
250 ml/8 fl oz crème fraîche
250 ml/8 fl oz poached rhubarb

Stem ginger cookies
55 g/2 oz stem ginger, finely chopped
2 ½ tablespoons golden syrup
2 tablespoons caster sugar
1 tablespoon soft brown sugar
85 g/3 oz unsalted butter
175 g/6 oz plain flour
1 tablespoon ground ginger

METHOD
* Using a slotted spoon, drain off most of the liquid from the rhubarb. If you have poached your rhubarb with ginger and really like ginger, leave the slices in it, but otherwise remove them. Put the poached rhubarb in a food processor and pulse three or four times, until smooth. Add the crème fraîche and stir the rhubarb puree through it. Check for sweetness. If too tart, add a couple of tablespoons of demerara sugar.
* Fill the bottom of a glass to about 5 cm/2 in with whole poached rhubarb (drain most of the liquid) and fill the remainder of the glass with the fool. Sprinkle with demerara sugar or other large brown sugar crystals for crunch. Serve with ginger cookies.
* For ginger cookies, preheat the oven to 180°C/355°F.
* Keep a little stem ginger aside for the top of the cookies.
* Heat the butter, sugar, syrup and stem ginger in a small saucepan. Stir the flour and ground ginger together and then add the melted butter mix. Bring the mixture together into a dough.
* Separate the dough into walnut sized pieces and place on a baking tray, an inch apart. Gently press them down with the back of a fork. Decorate with left over stem ginger and caster sugar.
* Bake for 15 to 18 minutes.

RHUBARB, APPLE AND CINNAMON CRUMBLE WITH NUTS

Serves 4

I love this combination in the early autumn. I think it's the perfect balance of fruit and nuts.

For the crumble

115 g/4 oz butter, cold
85 g/3 oz flour
85 g/3 oz demerara sugar
85 g/3 oz oatflakes (quick oats)
55 g/2 oz hazelnuts
55 g/2 oz pecans
2 teaspoons ground cinnamon
½ teaspoon allspice

For the filling

2 Bramley apples (or other tart, cooking apples, if unavailable)
1 orange, zest and juice, plus a little extra orange juice
55 g/2 oz demerara sugar
1 teaspoon ground cinnamon
4 large spoonfuls poached rhubarb drained of its juice or 4 sticks of rhubarb, cut into 2 cm/1 in pieces

METHOD

❋ Preheat the oven to 190°C/375°F.

❋ Using a food processor, pulse together the butter, flour, cinnamon and sugar. Then stir in the oatflakes. Set aside.

❋ Crush the nuts slightly in a plastic bag. Then roast them in a dry, non-stick frying pan until fragrant. Do not allow them to burn. Set aside to cool. Once cool, add them to the crumble mixture.

❋ Make a small amount of stewed apple. Peel, core and cut the apples into small pieces. Add the zest of the orange and the juice, as well as the cinnamon and demerara sugar. Cook, gently, until soft. Mash roughly with a fork.

❋ If you are using uncooked rhubarb, toss it in 55 g/2 oz of brown sugar and allow it to sit for 10 minutes to macerate a little. Then combine with the apple.

❋ If you are using cooked rhubarb, drain it of some of the liquid (but not all) and combine with the apple.

❋ Fill the bottom of a baking dish with the fruit. Spread the crumble-nut mixture on top and sprinkle over some brown sugar.

❋ Bake for 35 minutes or until bubbling and golden. Serve with cream or crème anglaise.

QUINCE JELLY, DAMSON JELLY, REDCURRANT AND LIME JELLY, CRABAPPLE JELLY, BLACKCURRANT JELLY

The method for making jellies is the same, whatever fruit you choose to use. The quantity of fruit also doesn't matter much, because it's the fruit juice you'll need to make the jelly, not the fruit itself.

* Put your fruit into a saucepan with the minimum amount of water necessary to encourage it to collapse and release its juice. For red and blackcurrants, and other soft fruit that could be until the bottom of the saucepan is just covered, for crabapples and quince, you will need a bit more—just enough that it doesn't catch on the bottom of the pan while the fruit is collapsing.

* Slowly bring the fruit to a simmer and cook until it is soft and collapses, releasing its juices. Put the collapsed fruit into a jelly bag and allow the juice to drip out in a cool place for several hours. Once you have separated the juice from the fruit, measure it out.

* You will need 450 g/1 lb of preserving sugar for each 570 ml/20 fl oz of fruit juice. Increase your quantities proportionately. You can sometimes get away with less sugar with high pectin fruit and can add some lemon or lime juice to make a less sweet, more tart jelly.

* If you are making black or redcurrant jelly, you must first remove the currants from their stalks. The easiest way to do this is to use a fork. Put a minimum of water, just enough to cover the bottom of the pan to prevent sticking, bring to a boil and then reduce to simmer gently, until collapsed. Once you have strained and measured the juice, warm it through and then add the warmed sugar. You can do this by spreading it in a large, dry, flat pan, and heating it gently in the oven for a few minutes—do not melt nor burn it. Add the sugar to the juice and bring slowly back to the boil and boil until the jelly sets when you put a teaspoonful of it onto a cold plate. In the case of blackcurrants, this will not be long—it can be a matter of a few minutes once returned to the boil.

* For redcurrants, you can add the juice of half a lime per 570 ml/20 fl oz of juice and the skin, peeled in wide strips and tied together (remove at the end of the cooking time). Keep checking for a set, as this can happen quickly.

* For crabapple jelly, wash and chop the crab apples, removing stalks and hard pieces. You can even add a couple of large Bramley apples if you are short of crabapples. Make sure that there's enough water so that the fruit does not catch on the bottom of the saucepan as it is cooking. Cook down to a pulp. Drain through a bag to retain the juice. Because crabapples have more pectin, you can use slightly less sugar than with currants, say. Anywhere between 345 and 450 g (12 oz–1 lb) will work fine. Add the strained juice of a couple of unwaxed lemons, and strips of the peel, tied together, and boil until set—once again, this is not an inexact science. Just keep testing it and don't go away, or it will surely turn to toffee!

* The method is the same for quince jelly and damson, both of which set easily.

Damson jam

Makes around 2.7 kg/6 lb of jam

INGREDIENTS

1.8 kg/4 lb damsons

1.35 kg/3 lb preserving sugar

METHOD

* Take the fruit and slit them with a knife. Layer them in a bowl with the sugar. Cover and leave overnight.

* The following day, put all the fruit and sugar in a saucepan and very slowly heat it, allowing the fruit to collapse. When liquid, bring to a boil and using a pair of spoons, remove the stones, which should float to the top.

* Test for setting quite quickly as it sets easily—you will almost certainly have to stop cooking the jam before you've found all the stones.

Morello cherry jam

Makes around 2.7 kg/6 lb of jam

INGREDIENTS

1.8 kg/4 lb morello cherries

½ pint redcurrant juice

1.35 kg/3 lb preserving sugar

METHOD

❄ Morello cherry jam is tiresome to get to set. But the results are delicious! Remove the stones from the cherries. Crush about half of them, then tie them up in a piece of muslin and add to the fruit and red currant juice in a saucepan. Simmer until tender.

❄ Warm the sugar by spreading it out in a baking dish or on a tray and sliding into a warm (not hot) oven for 10 minutes. The idea is not to cook the sugar, but to warm it so it does not lower the temperature of the juice to which it is being added. Add the sugar to the saucepan and stir until it is dissolved then boil rapidly until the jam sets when tested.

❄ Squeeze out and remove the stone bag.

CHAPTER 13

NEED-TO-KNOW BASICS

A NOTE ON FLOUR

I always use gluten free flour, but I recognise that the blend of ingredients in gluten free flour mixes varies widely around the world. They often tend to be drier than their conventional wheat counterpart, which means you many need to add a dash more liquid in recipes where you choose to use it.

A NOTE ON SALT AND PEPPER

Mostly, I use two kinds of salt. The first is a herb salt called Herbamare. It's an excellent product that works well in most savoury recipes. The second is Maldon salt—those beautiful, large flakes. Black pepper should always be freshly ground.

Chicken Stock

Makes approximately 8 litres/14 pints, but you can make less by adding less water and using a smaller saucepan

I make a very large saucepan of chicken stock once a week. This is where you can use up all your vegetable ends. During the rest of the week, I simply throw any leek, carrot and parsley ends into the freezer. When it's time to make stock, I add them to the pot straight from the freezer.

INGREDIENTS

1 giant stockpot
2 chicken carcasses or 1 turkey carcass
4 carrots, broken in half
4 leek ends
2 medium onions sliced in half
2 celery sticks
handful of parsley stalks
2 tablespoons black peppercorns
4 bay leaves
cold water to fill

METHOD

❋ Bring the saucepan slowly to the boil. Allow to simmer for 15 minutes, skim any foam that rises to the top and turn the heat down so that it is just simmering, little bubbles going blop, blop on the surface. Cover and cook for at least 2 hours. Sometimes I leave it all day.

❋ Drain your stock, keeping the liquid and throwing out the vegetables and bones. Return the stock to a clean saucepan and return the liquid to a boil. Skim off any solids that rise to the top and discard. Boil until reduced by one third to one half—the more you reduce it, the more intense the flavour will be. Cool and freeze for making soups and sauces.

Beef stock

Makes approximately 5 litres/9 pints

INGREDIENTS

2.3 kg/5 lb (approx.) beef bones

3 onions, chopped in half, unpeeled

1 head garlic, chopped in four

large handful of parsley, sage and thyme, tied together with string

2 leeks, roughly chopped

2 carrots, broken in half

2 stalks celery, roughly chopped

2 large tomatoes, roughly chopped

1 tablespoon black peppercorns

METHOD

✳ Preheat the oven to 200°C/400°F.

✳ Place the onions on the bottom of a large roasting tin. Add the garlic. Place the bones on top and add an inch of water to the pan. Roast in the oven for 45 minutes, until caramelised. Add more water if drying out.

✳ Fill your large stockpot about two-thirds full with 4–5 litres of cold water. Bring to a simmer. Add the roasted bones, onions and garlic, scraping the pan for any delicious brown bits. Add all remaining vegetables and herbs. Simmer, covered, for as long as possible—up to 6 hours.

✳ Drain the stock, keeping the liquid and throwing away the bones and vegetables. Return to the heat, skim off any solids that rise to the top and boil until reduced by half. Cool and freeze for later use.

BASIC WHITE SAUCE

Serves 4

INGREDIENTS

2 tablespoons butter

2 tablespoons plain flour

250 ml/8 fl oz milk

salt and freshly ground black pepper

½ teaspoon freshly grated nutmeg

2 tablespoons chopped parsley

115 g/4 oz sharp grated cheddar (optional, to add depth of flavour)

METHOD

✳ In a medium saucepan, heat the butter over medium-low heat until melted. Add the flour and stir until smooth. Over medium heat, cook until the mixture turns a light, golden sandy colour, about 6–7 minutes.

✳ Meanwhile, heat the milk in a separate pan until just about to boil. Add the hot milk to the butter mixture in a steady stream, whisking continuously until smooth. Bring to a boil. Simmer for 10 minutes, stirring, then remove from heat. Season with salt, pepper and nutmeg and stir in the parsley and a handful of sharp grated cheddar, if you like.

✳ Set aside in a warm place until ready to use.

MAYONNAISE

Makes about 250 ml/8 fl oz

When I was little, my favourite snack was a cold boiled potato dipped in globs of homemade mayonnaise. My mother no longer makes homemade mayonnaise and nor do I, unless it's a very special occasion. I find that Hellmann's made with olive oil is great for everyday use when mixed up with full fat yoghurt and lots of herbs. So you can substitute Hellmann's in any recipe that calls for mayonnaise, or you can follow this easy recipe to make your own, luxurious version.

INGREDIENTS
1 egg
¼ teaspoon salt
½ teaspoon dry mustard
¾ cup vegetable or hazelnut oil (I prefer the nut oil)
4 tablespoons extra virgin olive oil
1 tablespoon lemon juice or white wine vinegar

METHOD
❋ I prefer to use a hand blender to make mayonnaise. Put the egg, salt and mustard powder in a bowl and beat hard for a minute. Then, turn your blender to its lowest setting and slowly, drip, drip, drip your vegetable/nut oil into the egg mixture. Once it's all incorporated, add the olive oil in the same way. Don't rush this part or your mayonnaise will curdle. Once the mixture is thick and has absorbed all the oil, add vinegar or lemon juice to taste.
❋ Store in a closed jar in the fridge.

ELDERFLOWER CORDIAL

Makes about 1.5 litres/3 pints

Elderflower grows all through the hedgerows in Britain in early summer. Pretty and fragrant, it's such a great alternative to sugar in so many recipes that if you've got time, it's worth making a batch.

INGREDIENTS
30 elderflower heads
1.5 litres/53 fl oz boiling water
900 g/2 lb caster sugar
55 g/2 oz citric acid
2 unwaxed oranges, sliced
2 unwaxed lemons, sliced

METHOD
❋ Pick over the elderflower heads and remove any small insects or brown bits.
❋ Stir the sugar into the boiling water in a large bowl to make a syrup. Set aside to cool. Next, add the orange and lemon slices and the citric acid. Then press the elderflowers below the surface of the liquid.
❋ Set aside in the fridge. Stir occasionally. After 24 hours, strain the liquid through some muslin and transfer to sterilised bottles. Store in the refrigerator.

INDEX

ACKNOWLEDGEMENTS

Any cookery book is, by definition, a collaborative effort: of ideas; of palates; of inspiration; of memories. No single person can possibly dream up hundreds of food ideas, prepare them, plate them and produce mouth-watering photographs. It takes a team.

While my name may be on the cover of this book, it would not have been possible without the support of my husband, Chris, and the ongoing encouragement of my parents, James and Angela Sellick and their love for great food, beautiful gardens and the British countryside. I am hugely indebted to Leigh Clapp for countless hours of work to produce these stunning photographs. And finally, Tess Courage and Kate Wilson, who both work at Pashley Manor Gardens, without whom this book would not have come together at all. Their creativity, passion, energy and organisation ensured that this project kept marching along. Thank you.

ABOUT THE AUTHORS

Hattie Klotz is a British journalist who has lived in Canada for close to 20 years. She writes regularly on food, design and interesting people doing interesting things. Married and the mother to three young girls, she grew up in a beautiful house with stunning gardens, now open to the public, created by her parents in East Sussex, England.

Leigh Clapp is a professional photographer with more than 20 years' experience, primarily as a garden specialist photojournalist but also with interiors and travel. Leigh's work appears regularly in magazines, newspapers and books, both in the UK and abroad.

First published in 2017 by New Holland Publishers Pty Ltd

London • Sydney • Auckland

The Chandlery 50 Westminster Bridge Road London SE1 7QY United Kingdom

1/66 Gibbes Street Chatswood NSW 2067 Australia

5/39 Woodside Ave Northcote, Auckland 0627 New Zealand

www.newhollandpublishers.com.au

A record of this book is held at the British Library and the National Library of Australia.

ISBN: 9781742578743

Group Managing Director: Fiona Schultz

Publisher: Diane Ward

Project Editor: Liz Hardy

Designer: Lorena Susak

Production Director: James Mills-Hicks

Printer: HangTai Printing

10 9 8 7 6 5 4 3 2 1

Keep up with New Holland Publishers on Facebook

www.facebook.com/NewHollandPublishers